Combat Films
American Realism: 1945-1970

by
Steven Jay Rubin

Jefferson : McFarland
1981

Cover illustration by Michelle Gauthe

Library of Congress Cataloging in Publication Data

Rubin, Steven Jay, 1951-
Combat films.

Includes index.
1. War films — History and criticism.
2. Moving-pictures — United States — History.
I. Title.
PN1995.9.W3R8   791.43'09'09358   80-17022
ISBN 0-89950-013-7 (cloth)   ISBN 0-89950-014-5 (paper)

McFarland & Company, Inc., Publishers
Box 611, Jefferson, North Carolina, 28640

For dear old Mom,
who always has a smile,
a word of encouragement, and
the best Sunday night dinners in America

Acknowledgments

General Patton once said, "an Army is a team." Without my team, I could never have finished this book. Every writer is backed by a specialized group of people who contribute time, money, ideas and criticism. I was no different.

Without the help of the Hollywood community, this book would have been impossible. Much of the material is pulled from a series of interviews with film artists. Those with whom I could not meet in person sent letters and consented to review the manuscript. I am particularly indebted to Pierre Boulle, in Paris, who took time to edit a draft of the beginning of Chapter 6, and writer Harry Brown who kindly helped reshape the opening of Chapter 1.

Producer Frank McCarthy contributed a great deal of time and interest to the *Patton* chapter, as did John Sturges to *The Great Escape* write-up. I would also like to thank Robert Pirosh, Sy Bartlett and Beirne Lay, Jr., who contributed additional time. A full list of contributors is on page viii.

Without the advice, and criticism of my close friend Jeff Kalmick, I would probably still be writing. He early suggested that I cut the scope of this book and concentrate on eight films of the period.

I would also like to thank friends and relatives who so graciously took the time to read—offering their invaluable comments and criticism.

The library of the Academy of Motion Pictures, Arts and Sciences, was, indeed, my home for a full year. With the help of Mildred Simpson, Bonnie Rothbart, Marlene Medwin, and others, I was able to gather information on thirty American combat films and integrate its significance into my own research materials. They work tirelessly and have contributed a great deal of time and effort towards the preservation of the history of motion pictures. I salute their integrity.

I would also like to thank Irwin Shaw for his guidance and continuing interest in the manuscript.

Finally, I would like to thank my parents Evelyn and Joseph Rubin for giving me the opportunity and encouragement to write this book. Without them, I would not be here.

Steven Jay Rubin

Summer 1980, Los Angeles

Table of Contents

Contributors to This Book

Screenwriters. Robert Hardy Andrews*, Edward Anhalt*, Sy Bartlett*, Michael Blankfort*, Edward Blum*, W.R. Burnett*, Richard Carr*, John Gay*, Beirne Lay Jr.*, Robert Lewin*, Albert Maltz*, Wendell Mayes*, Richard Murphy*, Walter Newman, Edmund North*, Robert Pirosh*, William Roberts*, Ted Sherdeman*, Leonard Spiegelgass, Daniel Taradash*, Barry Trivers*, Peter Viertel*, Michael Wilson.

Novelists. Pierre Boulle, Harry Brown, Irwin Shaw*.

Directors. Delmer Daves*, Edward Dmytryk*, Tay Garnett*, Henry Hathaway*, Richard Goldstone*, Henry King*, Anatole Litvak*, Leslie Martinson*, Lewis Milestone*, David Miller*, Gerd Oswald*, Robert Relyea*, Mark Robson, George Seaton*, Franklin J. Schaffner*, John Sturges*, J. Lee Thompson*, Don Siegel*, Billy Wilder, Elmo Williams*, Robert Wise*, Fred Zinneman*.

Producers. Carl Foreman*, Brynie Foy*, Edmund Grainger*, Nunnally Johnson*, Stanley Kramer*, Frank McCarthy*, Martin Rackin, Aaron Rosenberg*, Milton Sperling*.

Cinematographers. William Clotheir*, Burnett Guffey*.

Stuntman. Bud Ekins*.

Actors. Dana Andrews, Richard Conte, James Garner*, James Mason, Burgess Meredith, Lawrence Montaigne*, Lloyd Nolan*, Gregory Peck, Paul Picerni, Cliff Robertson, Jud Taylor*, Marshall Thompson.

*Interviewed personally by the author.

viii

Introduction

This is not a story of war. Neither is it a history of films about war. It is instead the story of a group of film makers who set out to achieve the impossible, to present the story of warfare without the glory or the manufactured heroics, the very ingredients that had always lured thrill-seeking audiences into the theaters.

This book covers the period between the end of World War II and the beginning of the 1970s, during which film makers strove to find and present the truth about war. It uncovers those new attitudes and influences by looking over the shoulders of the men who were involved in the production of these films.

This is an anthology, there being eight stories about film making. Many of the films are well known and some have always appeared on "best picture" lists of all time. However, I have not chosen the films primarily for their greatness. The interesting common denominator is that they each have a unique story to tell, a story of creative frustration, of artistic perseverance, and of final victory. Here is the blow-by-blow account of a film genre that is only now gaining the respect and admiration it has always deserved.

Who were these men who made the war movies and who provide the focus of this book? Many of them were veterans of World War II.

Producer Darryl F. Zanuck who personally produced more World War II films than anyone, while a producer and studio executive at 20th Century-Fox, was a colonel in the U.S. Army Signal Corps who saw action in North Africa and Western Europe.

Milton Sperling, who later produced such films as *Merrill's*

Marauders, The Courtmartial of Billy Mitchell, and *The Battle of the Bulge*, was a Marine second lieutenant attached to a photographic unit on Guadalcanal and Tarawa.

Prolific director Lewis Milestone, forever tied to the combat film genre, was a veteran of the Signal Corps in World War I, and although he was stationed in Washington, D.C., he learned a great deal from the actual combat footage that reeled through his office.

During World War II, many Hollywood artists and craftsmen were assigned stateside to the two major Signal Corps Photographic Centers at Astoria, Long Island, and Culver City, California. Future directors like Richard Goldstone (*No Man Is an Island*), David Miller (*The Flying Tigers,* and *Captain Newman, M.D.*) and Carl Foreman (*The Guns of Navarone,* and *The Victors*) were exposed to massive quantities of combat footage that they incorporated into hundreds of quality government backed documentary films that covered every subject from the arts of camouflage to the treatment of venereal disease.

And there were those who saw war at first hand. Tough, outspoken director Samuel Fuller, who went on to film *The Steel Helmet, Merrill's Marauders,* and *The Big Red One*, was a platoon sergeant in the First Infantry Division.

Writers Sy Bartlett and Beirne Lay, Jr., who collaborated on both the novel and screenplay of *Twelve O'Clock High*, served as officers with the U.S. Eighth Air Force in Europe. Bartlett would later create films like *Pork Chop Hill, Strategic Air Command*, and *The Outsider*. Britisher J. Lee Thompson, who directed *The Guns of Navarone*, was another flyer, of Lancaster bombers with the Royal Air Force.

Cinematographer William Clotheir, who worked on both *Merrill's Marauders* and *The Devil's Brigade*, had been a Paramount Pictures newsreel cameraman stationed in Madrid during the Spanish Civil War. Before he was inducted into the Ninth Air Force to film documentaries with such directors as William Wyler and John Sturges, Clotheir was filming German Stuka dive bombers raids on the Spanish capital. Wyler would later use his experience to film the classic Air Force documentary, *The Memphis Belle*, while Sturges went on to create *Never So Few, The Great Escape, Ice Station Zebra,* and *The Eagle Has Landed*.

Director Anatole Litvak spent much of pre-Pearl Harbor World War II being hounded by the German S.S. and Gestapo. He was producing French films up until the invasion of the Low Countries in May 1940 and later in the United States, where he directed the controversial anti-Nazi film, *Confessions of a Nazi Spy* as well as *Decision before Dawn.*

The latter film, an engrossing study of the last days of the Third Reich, that was filmed in the ruins of postwar Germany, was written by Peter Viertel, an American officer attached to the Office of Strategic Services (O.S.S.). While with the headquarters of the U.S. Seventh Army, Viertel learned at first hand the espionage story later dramatized in *Decision before Dawn.*

Authors Irwin Shaw and Henry Brown were both war correspondents, the former using his experiences to write one of the great novels of the war, *The Young Lions*, which became a 20th Century-Fox film in 1958. Brown's novel *A Walk in the Sun* would become the final combat film produced during the actual war.

Like Samuel Fuller, writer Robert Pirosh was also a combat infantryman, a master sergeant in the 35th Infantry Division. Pirosh would later write three realistic studies of war: *Battleground, Go for Broke,* and *Hell Is for Heroes*, the latter directed by Don Siegel, a wartime documentary film maker.

Screenwriter James Ruffin Webb, who coauthored *Pork Chop Hill* and who later wrote a preliminary draft on *Patton*, was himself an officer with General Lloyd Fredendall's II Corps in North Africa, a unit leader commanded by Patton himself.

While Fuller, Pirosh and Webb were marching across Western Europe, writer Robert Lewin was riding a tank in the Italian Campaign. He later became a company commander of a tank destroyer unit near San Pietro (where director John Huston was filming a classic combat documentary) and after the war wrote still another excellent combat film, the seldom seen *The Bold and the Brave*, which was released in 1956 by RKO Pictures.

Aside from being qualified to film an accurate portrait of World War II, many of the directors went even further, developing an obsession for minute detail and realism. While filming *Patton* in Spain in 1969, director Franklin Schaffner and his crew spent days trying to figure out how to simulate the recoil of a tank firing dummy ammunition.

On location for *The Desert Fox*, in 1950, director Henry Hathaway searched so hard for the scene of Rommel's encounter with strafing Spitfires that he actually found pieces of the Field Marshal's staff car along the side of a road in Normandy.

Whatever their background or obsession, they all fought the same creative battles with the studio executives, the financial backers, the advertising and promotion departments and the scoffers who constantly demanded entertaining, money making films. And no matter how successful the films later became, they still left behind a group of sometimes disillusioned, sometimes exultant creative artists who had given their all for realism. This book is dedicated to their willpower.

I

Filming History, Not Heroics

The combat film was always a natural entertainment medium. Even as the first cameras were being hand cranked, film makers were planning battle action for the silver screen. Soon after the Spanish American War in 1898, an innovative producer created what was to be the first combat film — a recreation of the naval battle off Manila. It was filmed entirely in a wash basin with a moving backdrop, paper ships and drifting cigar smoke. The quest for realism had begun.

Nearly sixty years ago, pioneer film maker David Wark Griffith, at work on the moving Civil War sequences for his masterwork, *The Birth of a Nation*, spoke of his own growing obsession for realism. He strongly felt that such a desire to film the truth would increase the very popularity of films themselves.

"We will be able to teach history in the future through the film medium," he said. "Realism will be a key element in the historical film, for the public will not settle for less."

Griffith was correct, especially in the realm of documentary films where multi-segment series like *Victory at Sea, You Are There,* and *The World at War* have enabled contemporary students of history to study the past in moving picture form.

Still, while the later feature films, released to theaters, included many of the realistic elements of the war documentaries, on the whole, they strayed from the true portrait predicted by Griffith. In satisfying the public's desire for adventure, romance, action and pathos, the feature films of the last half century have for the most part sacrificed a most important element of realism. Only in certain individual cases have they succeeded.

During World War II, Hollywood's dream factories created hundreds of motion pictures, many of them government backed training films that explained the goals and technicalities of fighting a modern global war. There were perhaps only half a hundred combat films in the classic sense, films that explored the war from a purely military perspective. Many of these were outright propaganda films that emphasized, early in the war, a "victory in defeat" philosophy.

These interesting productions were usually symbolized by a dirty, tired American soldier, who, like Robert Taylor in the 1942 film *Bataan*, fought like hell to stop the onrushing Japanese. One cannot forget that final scene with Taylor, the sole survivor of his patrol, holding off a large unit of enemy soldiers with a blistering wave of lead from his heavy machine gun, smoke gradually obscuring the scene, his fate tragically sealed.

Similiar sequences were repeated in dozens of films like *Manila Calling, Wake Island, Edge of Darkness*, and *The Flying Tigers*. The geography might be different, the branch of service or the enemy various, but the outcome was always the same. Glory in defeat, or as the narrator says at the conclusion of *Wake Island* (1942), after a Marine garrision on a Pacific Island has been totally wiped out,

"This is not the end!"

But the tide turned, especially after the battle of Midway, El Alamein and Stalingrad, and motion pictures became much more confident of final victory.

The grim harrassed Robert Taylor was replaced by a more gutsy outspoken soldier such as Humphrey Bogart who commanded an American Grant tank named Lulubelle in director Zoltan Korda's 1943 film, *Sahara*. It was a movie filled to the brim with confidence.

The story was no different from that of *Bataan* and yet the film's entire texture was new and enlivening. The grim forebording atmosphere so apparent in the foggy Philippine jungles in *Bataan* was gone. Instead, there was the broiling desert landscape of Libya, a solitary tank and ten forgotten men holding off a German mechanized battalion. The difference? They win.

As propaganda and glory were left behind, realism became a prime element in the American combat film. To keep pace, Hollywood, late in the war, abandoned the early symbolism and returned to the themes so present in the late 1930's when *The Grapes of Wrath* and *I Was a Fugitive from a Chain Gang* were telling it like it was.

1

Bullets or Ballads

Lewis Milestone's 1946 film *A Walk in the Sun* was the last of the wartime combat films. It tells a simple story about a platoon of American soldiers who hit the beach at Salerno, in sunny Italy, and who take a little walk in the sun. In its tense, exciting 117 minutes, director Milestone gives us an extraordinarily intimate portrait of men in war.

Here is the throbbing story of the foot slogging infantryman who, as medical corpsman McWilliams (Sterling Holloway) points out, "Never sees Nothing!" While the generals plan their grand strategy, initiate their careful tactical deployments and prepare for their map and table oriented warfare, it is the infantryman who must fight for every yard of dirt. In *A Walk in the Sun* the objective is an Italian farm house six miles from the beach.

In the film, as an early illustration of the new emphasis on realism, the enemy is seldom seen. When the German Army does appear, it remains hidden behind the machines of war. At the beginning of the film, the platoon's lieutenant is mortally wounded by a shell that appears out of nowhere, smashing against the side of the landing craft and scattering shrapnel in all directions.

Later, McWilliams is cut down by a lone enemy fighter plane that appears briefly, killing the medic and wounding two other soldiers, and then flies back into anonymity. When the platoon later destroys an enemy armored car, there are no visible enemy casualties. Milestone's camera simply takes in a smouldering half track. Even the unit's final objective, the Italian farmhouse, is only a building surrounded by orchards. There is no clue to its military identity.

A Walk in the Sun was the product of an American Army

Staff Sergeant named Harry Brown who in 1942 was sent to London to work on the British edition of *Yank* magazine. Brown, who had served with the Army Corps of Engineers at Fort Belvoir, Virginia, before joining *Yank* in New York, was jubilant about his new assignment.

"I wasn't sure what my duties would be," he later remembered, "but I thought for sure that I'd be a field reporter going on commando raids, Wilhelmshaven bombings, and other cloak and dagger operations."

Before Brown left New York, he signed a contract with the publishing firm of McGraw-Hill to write a book called *Sergeant Brown Reporting*. The idea was that for every mission he undertook for *Yank*, he'd write one version for the magazine and one for the book.

But much to his chagrin, things didn't work out that way. He found himself trapped as a deskman, rewriting material that the actual correspondents were turning in, and grinding out such nondescript items as *A Week of War*, and *Artie Greengroin, PFC*.

This mundane routine lasted throughout 1943 and every once in a while Brown would get a letter from his publisher inquiring, expectantly, about the progress of the book.

Say Brown, "Towards the end of the year these letters had built up such a feeling of guilt in me that I felt I had to give them something. Things were going from bad to worse at *Yank*. The tensions between the New York and London offices were unbelievable. Finally, when they wished a new major on us, the editor of the London edition and I both resigned."

With a great deal of time on his hands, Brown began to nose around London, trying to fit himself into another outfit.

"I was on per diem and did not have to live in the Army barracks. So, what with one thing and another, I figured I'd better discharge my debt to McGraw-Hill. I sat down in the top room of the house I'd taken on Brompton Square, and in two weeks, working only in the evenings, I turned out a novel. I called it *A Walk in the Sun.*'"

How do these men of the 45th "Texas Division" survive their particular brand of hell on Salerno Beach? Sergeant Brown gave them a slogan, "Nobody Dies!"

It was a tough cynical cliché in this platoon of footsore

Top: *Rivera (Richard Conte), Porter (Herbert Rudley) and Tyne (Dana Andrews) in the "Italy" of the dry San Fernando Valley, California, 1944.* Bottom: *Sergeant Harry Brown as he looked in 1944 when he wrote* A Walk in the Sun *in London.*

combat veterans. They knew it was a lie. They saw their lieutenant get hit in the face, their sergeant crumple full of machine gun slugs, their last commander go out of his mind. But to come out alive they had to fight off panic with wisecracks, pull their shattered ranks together and then gamble their final ounce of strength in an all out assault.

Who were these tired soldiers? Brown created them, remembering many of the letters he had once read while manning the desk at *Yank*. In the film's opening actor Burgess Meredith introduced the men.

"There was Tyne [Dana Andrews], who never had much urge to travel. Providence, Rhode Island, may not be much as cities go but it was all he wanted, a one town man; Rivera [Richard Conte], Italian American, likes opera and would like a wife and kid, plenty of kids; Friedman [George Tyne], lathe operator and amateur boxing champ, New York City; Windy [John Ireland], minister's son, Canton, Ohio, used to take long walks alone and just think...

"Sergeant Ward [Lloyd Bridges], a farmer who knows his soil, a good farmer; McWilliams [Sterling Holloway], first aid man, slow, Southern, dependable; Archenbeau [Norman Lloyd], platoon scout and prophet, talks a lot but he's all right; Porter, Sergeant Porter [Herbert Rudley], he well, he has a lot on his mind, a lot on his mind; Tranella [Danny Desmond] speaks two languages, Italian and Brooklyn. And a lot of other men..."

Brown sent the first draft of *A Walk in the Sun* to McGraw-Hill in September 1943. Back came a letter saying, in effect, "It's a nice job, but you seem to have forgotten that we're a nonfiction house."

Fortunately, McGraw-Hill released Brown from his commitment by offering the novel to Knopf in return for the $500 advance they had given Brown. The Sergeant soon received an enthusiastic letter from Blanche Knopf telling him that they were quite pleased with the book and that it would be published the following June.

A Walk in the Sun was extraordinarily timely as it was published just a week after D-Day in Normandy. Sales were good and the novel quickly gained fourth place on the *New York Times* best seller list.

While the novel was receiving good critical notices

throughout the United States, motion picture director Lewis
Milestone was in Los Angeles recuperating from a five week bout
with a ruptured appendix.

Of all Hollywood directors who came to prominence during
the thirties and forties, Lewis Milestone was perhaps the most
adept at filming realistic combat scenes. Born in Russia in 1895, he
had grown up in the town of Kishnev, the capital of Bessarabia, attended school in Germany and later emigrated to the United States
where he served in the U.S. Army Signal Corps during World War
I.

Assigned to the Photographic Division (he had previously
worked in a theatrical photographer's studio for $7 a week),
Milestone was transferred to Washington, D.C., where he worked
on training films with directors Victor Fleming and Josef Von
Sternberg.

Emerging from the Army, Milestone left for Hollywood to
work with Jesse Hampton Productions. Hampton, one of
Milestone's wartime associates, offered him a position in his cutting room at $20 a week. He soon began editing films for director
Henry King.

In 1925, Milestone made his directorial debut at Warner
Brothers on *Seven Sinners*, based on his own original idea which
he cowrote with a young screenwriter named Darryl F. Zanuck.

While Milestone was a very flexible director in terms of subject matter, the outstanding success of his 1930 film, *All Quiet on
the Western Front*, frequently tied him to the combat film genre.
While his later films were less impressive thematically, they never
lost the true humanity that characterized his beloved study of the
First World War and its effect on a group of young German
soldiers. *All Quiet on the Western Front* would affect an entire
generation of new directors who were awestruck by the film's im-
passioned outcry against war and its horrors. Director Don Siegel
would never forget the film and his contribution to the combat
film genre, *Hell Is for Heroes* (1962), later explored similar
ground.

As director Karel Reisz observes, "While Milestone's
primary emphasis is always on the emotions of his characters, he
also conveys the full vastness of the tragedy in his large battle
scenes. Milestone's eloquent device of tracking the camera across a

coming advance of troops or tanks generates an overwhelming sense of impersonal horror.

"Milestone brings to his war films the essential grasp of the big situation and the willingness to put over huge overwhelming effects directly. He faces the devastating moments of horror and does not sentimentalize the occasional moments of peace and beauty. To each, his intensely personal super realistic style of conveying emotional stresses in compositions gives at once an individual poetry and universal validity."

Few directors have ever received such comment on their work in the combat film genre. It was this type of critical acceptance that enabled Milestone to develop his peculiar craft in a number of future films, including *A Walk in the Sun.*

Following his Academy Award winning work on *All Quiet on the Western Front*, Milestone, however, avoided the war drama, as did Hollywood in the pacifist thirties, to concentrate on films like *The Front Page*, and *Of Mice and Men*. The attack on Pearl Harbor reawakened Milestone's interest and abilities in the combat film genre.

In 1943, he directed *Edge of Darkness*, an Errol Flynn adventure about the Norwegian resistance against the Nazis, a theme similar to that of his next film, *The North Star*, which told of the Russian resistance against the Nazis. One year later, he completed *The Purple Heart*, a gripping drama of American flyers who are captured and tortured by the Japanese for taking part in the Doolittle Raid of 1942.

A chance encounter with producer Samuel Bronston opened the way to *A Walk in the Sun*. Bronston wanted Milestone to get away from the studio system and work on an independent project of his choice. The finished film would be released by United Artists. This appealed to the director, who was weary of the major studio bureaucracy.

Bronston invited Milestone to continue his convalescence in New York where Bronston was forming a small group of independent film makers, including French exiles René Clair and Julian Duvivier.

Recalled Milestone, "They were really living it up at the Waldorf Astoria where everybody had a beautiful suite of his own. Bronston sure knew how to spend money."

The producer's opulence worried Milestone, but the director was in no position to complain. Given a luxurious suite at the Sherry Netherlands, across from the Central Park he mourned the loss of his appendix and began to search for a new film project.

Samuel Bronston was a financial wizard who had recently distinguished himself in Europe, before the war, as a film salesman. Like Milestone, he was a native of Russia who came from a family of nine boys and girls, all reared and educated in France and all distinguished in law, medicine, art and music. Five of his brothers were doctors and his sister Carol Bronte became a famous opera singer.

Bronston started out to become a surgeon but fainted at his first autopsy, so he took to music and played the flute with the Paris orchestra to pay his tuition at the Sorbonne.

As a successful film salesman, he gained prominence in Europe and later migrated to Hollywood, before World War II broke out, where he began a career in film making. In 1942, he produced *The Adventures of Martin Eden*, a Jack London story that starred a very young Glenn Ford. This was followed by *The Jack London Story*, which starred Michael O'Shea and Susan Hayward. In 1943, he was already an established independent, associated with United Artists, which would release his next project.

In July 1944, the Zeppo Marx Agency in New York sent Milestone a copy of Harry Brown's *A Walk in the Sun*. Milestone read the little book and the accompanying reviews and told Bronston, "I like it Sam. Buy it and I'll do it!" It was as simple as that.

It was only during the bargaining for the novel's rights that Milestone began to keenly suspect Bronston's precarious financial status, as he recalls:

"By now, I realized that Bronston owned no oil wells. He was not a wealthy man, and since his mode of living including putting up two other directors besides myself, I wondered how long it could last. The thing to do, I decided, was to move in, get the story done and get out fast. Because it looked as though the sky would soon fall in."

Bronston continued to assure Milestone that everything was in order. He purchased the film rights from Knopf and began to make arrangements to secure the $700,000 budget of *A Walk in the Sun*.

Two weeks later, Milestone met screenwriter Robert Rossen in the lobby of the Sherry Netherlands, each surprised by the other's presence in New York.

"What great timing!" exclaimed Milestone who had worked with Rossen on *Edge of Darkness*. "I've got this little book I just picked up. I'm working with Sam Bronston, an independent producer. If you want in, okay. But we're leaving any minute for Los Angeles. I want to warn you that this has to be a fast job. We've got to work very hard on this thing. Make a deal with Bronston and then we'll fly out to the coast together."

On his way out, Rossen hesitated, "You said Bronston is an independent producer?"

"Yes," said Milestone, "does that bother you?"

"I'm just wondering whether the money is good." Rossen wasn't nitpicking. He was simply fed up with Hollywood. He had recently moved back to New York, had enrolled the youngsters in school and decided that he was well rid of Hollywood politics.

Robert Rossen was one of Hollywood's most promising young writers, and a future producer. He was a native New Yorker and a onetime boxer from Manhattan's lower east side. The grandson of a rabbi and the nephew of a Hebrew poet, Rossen's childhood experiences bred in him a rebellious nature which later saw outlet on the screen.

After attending Columbia University, he turned to writing. His theatrical career started, though, when at the age of 21 he directed Richard Maibaum's play, *The Tree*, in 1929. His second directorial effort was another Maibaum play (Maibaum later became a screenwriter), *Birthright*, and from then on he turned to playwriting. Rossen's first success was *The Body Beautiful*, which was produced in 1934 and which brought him quickly to the attention of Warner Brothers and director Mervyn Leroy. Two years later, he came west and began writing at Warners.

"Through the years in Hollywood," Rossen later recalled, "I've always had the feeling that one of the things wrong with it was a too great separation between the creator of the material and his audience. The playwright, the artist in most creative forms, lives by the direct reaction of the public to his finished work. Too many motion pictures, however, are sifted through the man sitting in the front office.

"I personally felt I had to get at that audience or quit pictures. And after half a dozen scripts, I did quit (in 1944-1945) and took my family to New York...."

With Bronston's financial backing, Rossen was quickly put to work on *A Walk in the Sun*. Both Rossen and Milestone were confident that their virtual independence would insulate them from any front office tampering and help creat a unique war story. This was not to be the, by now, somewhat traditional propaganda film, waving the flag, espousing the cause of final victory. Brown's grim narrative was to be retained, practically verbatim. It was to be a pointedly limited perspective saga of the foot soldier, period!

Since they had worked together on *Edge of Darkness*, the precedent enabled them to dispense with personality clashes and allow them to develop the story with a common sense of purpose. Both were excited about returning to work and their enthusiasm spilled over into a project that could easily have turned into just another American combat film.

Rossen began writing in an office at the Samuel Goldwyn Studios in Hollywood—the virtual haven of independent productions. Producer Bronston had agreed that speed was important, especially since there was talk that the war in Europe would be over in December. Milestone continually relayed the message to Rossen.

As the director recalled, "I didn't want to be hard to get along with, but I'd made a deal for a flat sum of money, and the quicker I got through with it, the better it would be for all of us."

In transforming Brown's novel to the screen, Rossen took advantage of the author's lucid style. The 160 page book was straightforward in construction and allowed Rossen to retain the basic narrative in its original form. The screenwriter was also able to transfer whole passages containing Brown's own dialogue directly to the screen. In fact, everybody later agreed that Brown's novel was practically a workable screenplay.

Rossen made only two minor changes in the final draft of *A Walk in the Sun*. He promoted Corporal Tyne to Sergeant in the role later portrayed by Dana Andrews, and he strengthened the part of Private "Windy" Craven (John Ireland), the soldier who composes letters aloud to his sister.

One of the script's outstanding characteristics is the sheer amount of dialogue. One reviewer later criticized the film on those very grounds, remarking that "the chief stumbling block in the film was its over indulgence in talk for its own sake."

Nonetheless, talkativeness became an integral part of the film, as it was in the novel. In an early passage, Brown writes, "Talking was a form of bravado. If a man said something, no matter what it was, it seemed to him that he was saying: "Here I am, very calm, very collected. Nothing's going to happen to me. The rest of the company's going to be wiped out, but nothing's going to happen to me. See, I can talk. I can form sentences. Do you think I could make conversations if I knew I was going to die?"

In a Los Angeles Times interview in 1945, Lewis Milestone also defended the abnormal amount of dialogue.

"The big effect," he told reporters, "was to externalize the thoughts and feelings of men in action. Every soldier talked, and through his dialogue we learned what was going on in his mind. My reaction to the criticism was that you gave articulation to what they would have said, if they could have said it. This was the quality that Harry Brown got into it and that was the quality I wanted to keep in the film."

Rossen, working around the clock, finished the first draft shooting script in just one week. But Milestone soon noticed that, even with the unifying elements provided by Private Craven's oral letters which often served as a practical narration, something was missing, an important factor that could elevate the project and, as Milestone hoped, "take it out of the category of the run-of-the-mill war film."

Milestone, recalling some research he had done on *The North Star*, remembered some scenes in which Russian veterans of various wars were being demobilized without benefit of the brief humanitarian stops at a halfway house, a veteran's hospital, or an institution similar to those that exist in the United States.

If the Russian soldier had been crippled by the war, society assumed no responsibility for him. They made no concessions; he could stand on a street corner selling satchels for all they cared.

Milestone remembered that these crippled vagabonds often sang of their experiences while playing a musical instrument like the balalaika.

"If we can somehow use that device," he told Rossen, "then

we can dramatize all of Harry's material without a typical narration. In the final film, Milestone's use of the ballad as a unifying element gave the film a unique cinematic structure.

The plan was to use the ballads, but as a narrative device. There would be no singer in the cast. The pair thumbed through the book, marking off all the plot elements they wanted to dramatize in ballad form. They found ten, more than they wanted, but both of them felt that the ballads represented a truly original approach.

Bronston agreed and immediately hired lyricist Millard Lampell to write the ballads. Musician/composer Earl Robinson, whose deep voice was quite distinctive and Western enough to symbolize the Texas Division, joined Lampell, putting the words to music. In the interest of economy, Robinson was also hired to play and sing the finished ballads.

Meanwhile, Milestone had begun shooting the exteriors at Agoura Ranch in the San Fernando Valley, which resembled the hinterland of Italy.

Instead of opening the film with the typical credits sequence, Milestone chose to begin with his first ballad. He felt that it would be an arresting way to introduce the film.

After a picture of Harry Brown's novel appears on the screen, the film opens with narrator Burgess Meredith.

"This book tells a story that happened long ago, way back in Nineteen Hundred and Forty Three, when the lead platoon of the Texas Division hit the beach at Salerno, in sunny Italy. It tells of Sergeant Tyne..."

Milestone's camera than focuses on the marching figure of Dana Andrews, while in the background the audience hears the soft refrain of "Over Hill, Over Dale." Meredith finishes his description of the platoon by simply saying, "Here's a song about them," a cue that led directly to the voice of Earl Robinson.

While Rossen continued to polish the script, Milestone kept a daily eye on the newspapers, scanning the war news for any interesting idea that he could incorporate into the film.

Facing page: *Sergeant Tyne (Dana Andrews) stops to chat with Private "Windy" Craven (John Ireland), the man who composes letters aloud to his sister.* — A Walk in the Sun *(20th Century-Fox, 1945).*

In late December 1944, during the climactic Battle of the Bulge, which extended the war in Europe for five months, Milestone discovered an interesting article, written by UPI correspondent Collie Small.

It was a dispatch from Germany. Small had come across a Brooklyn GI talking to a dead German. The kid had just missed the final payoff and was full of the wonder of being alive, while the big blond German lay dead.

For the film, Milestone asked actor George Offerman (portraying Tinker) to recreate the incident. In the scene, Tinker is standing on a burning armored car talking to a body.

"You know Al," he says, "you there, you got no right to squawk. You made up for one of ours. Look at you. You're deader than a mackerel. Look at me. I still got a whole life to look forward to. Just because of you, I got a tour of Europe that don't cost me a thing, and what did you get? You got shot in a barnyard, that's what." And when another soldier steps over, Tinker just looks at him.

"Just having a little talk with Al here." With one last look at the corpse, he walked away.

After Milestone had been shooting for a week on location, Bronston phoned from New York with terrible news. The bank that had promised to finance the picture had changed its mind.

It was a disastrous blow to Milestone and the whole crew. The production was already $45,000 in debt.

The director was faced with the choice of losing everything he had done so far or scraping up some money to meet the immediate costs, while Bronston tried to promote a new loan. In desperation, Milestone put some of his own money into the production and managed to borrow enough to keep going day by day. He soon found himself working all day on the set and then spending most of the night trying to raise money.

Bronston called again with the reassurance that he was about to close a loan deal with a Chicago bank. He called again the next day to announce another more imminent arrangement. A group of Chicago financiers was willing to advance $200,000 at 6 percent interest plus a bonus of 15 percent and 40 percent of the picture's profits. It was a terrible giveaway, and when the Chicago bankers heard about the preposterous deal they withdrew their

"Take it easy," says Tyne (Dana Andrews) to Porter (Herbert Rudley), who no longer has the mental strength to command. — A Walk in the Sun *(20th Century-Fox, 1945).*

proferred loan of $300,000. Bankrupt and defeated, Bronston walked away from the picture, leaving Milestone in the middle of the San Fernando Valley with an army of hungry soldiers.

Milestone immediately flew to Chicago to see David O'Hara, who headed the Chicago financiers.

Recalls Milestone, "O'Hara met me at the airport and said that he agreed that the original deal would have to be rewritten. 'Look,' I told him, 'I will agree to the rewriting of the deal, but a new arrangement has to be beneficial to both parties. The terms you gave Bronston are ridiculous. I'm not going to stand for any usury on your part. I'm willing, though, to make sacrifices. I have fifty percent of the picture, so let's bring our lawyers into this and work out a reasonable deal.'"

The hardnosed bargaining attitude which Milestone brought to Chicago paid off. O'Hara agreed to put up the necessary $750,000 in finish the picture on terms agreeable to Milestone. His production bankrolled, Milestone still had major problems with which to deal.

The finished script had been submitted to Washington for routine approval and the Army wanted some changes made, particularly in the final scene in the film where the platoon launches a World War I bayonet charge on the heavily defended farm house. The military wondered where the platoon's bazookas were.

Milestone explained that there weren't any. If there had been, the infantrymen could have waited out of range and blown the farmhouse to bits.

"And then where would our story be? said Milestone.

The Army stood firm. "That," they said, "is why we use bazookas. So you had better use them."

Without authorization from the Army, the film could not go into general release, so Milestone had Rossen write bazookas into the story, with a twist that satisfied the Army and saved the last scene in the picture.

Tyne's platoon does have bazookas but during an armored engagement they are trained against a group of tanks and armored cars and all the ammunition is used up. When the unit moves against the farmhouse, they have good reason to leave the empty bazookas behind.

A Walk in the Sun was officially completed on January 5, 1945, with no less than 11 Millard Lampell ballads, all sung by Earl Robinson. When Milestone showed the finished film to some of his friends, producer Sam Spiegel was the first to comment.

"We think you're insane. You guys have a wonderful war melodrama, and yet you keep interrupting the damned thing with these silly ballads. Every time you have a ballad, the action comes to a dead stop."

The director listened to the criticism but refused to consider cutting any of the ballads. He wanted to await the reaction from the theater audience.

"Thanks for the advice," Milestone told Spiegel, "I appreciate your concern. But the beauty of doing an independent picture is that you don't have to listen to anybody. Not even your friends."

At the first sneak preview, Milestone, to his dismay, was

aware of a wave of grumbling from the younger members of the audience during the ballad sequences and he was suddenly afraid that his friends had been right.

Spiegel was the first to approach him after the screening. "We warned you. We told you people wouldn't go for the ballads. Why do you insist on keeping them in?"

Milestone was still unable to accept the thought that his picture sense had erred to such a degree. He wandered around the lobby soliciting opinions from the audience. A group of young people who were leaving the theater caught Milestone's attention.

Milestone ran after them. "Excuse me," he called, "were you by any chance discussing the music in the film you just saw?"

"Yes!" they chorused.

"Obviously," Milestone hesitated, "...Obviously there was something about it which you didn't like. Would you mind telling me what it was? I produced the film."

"Oh, we loved the picture," said one teenaged boy, "but where did you get that hillbilly singer?"

Ah ha! It wasn't the ballads that had bothered them at all. It was squarish Earl Robinson. Relieved, Milestone thanked the young people for their advice but lamented that Robinson was the best he could find.

Satisfied that the ballads were still a good film device, Milestone nonetheless reduced their number from eleven to six. He realized that too many might prove intolerable to the nation's young film goers.

Only a few days after the sneak preview, Milestone was confronted with a new, more complex problem. With Samuel Bronston off the picture, he was told that United Artists had canceled their release agreement. Later, Milestone was told the true story, that UA had already committed themselves to Lester Cowan's *The Story of GI Joe* and didn't want to compete with their own product. It was another untimely blow. Milestone once more flew to Chicago to see his bankroller David O'Hara about a plan.

"With your permission," he told O'Hara, "I will run the film for Darryl Zanuck at 20th Century-Fox. I know Darryl and I think I can get a release from him that will be even better than the United Artists' deal."

"Do you think you can swing it?" asked O'Hara.

"I promise nothing, but I'll try," replied Milestone.

O'Hara agreed and Milestone flew back to Hollywood the following day to see Zanuck. He didn't relish the thought of sacrificing his independance by going back to a major studio, but there was no longer any choice in the matter.

Zanuck, though, the production head of 20th Century-Fox, could offer little encouragement.

"You know I have nothing to do with the releasing end of the business," Zanuck told him, "that's all in the hands of the New York office."

Milestone was imperturbable. "I know, Darryl, but a good word from you is all I ask. If you recommend it, I know I can get a screening in New York."

Zanuck relented and two days later Milestone sent a print over to Zanuck's home where the production executive kept a private screening room. As luck would have it, the film was scheduled to be shown on April 12, 1945, the day President Franklin Delano Roosevelt died and an entire nation went into mourning.

Milestone waited in suspense for an hour for Darryl to push the button on the projector. The president's death had hit him very deeply and he was not in the mood for a war picture. Finally, Zanuck decided to run it.

"We started the thing, at last," recalls Milestone, "and when the film was finished Zanuck was very pleased. He told Milestone that he would recommend the film. "But you'll have to go to New York personally to run a print for them. And Milly, you have too many ballads. I love them, but you've got to take some out."

Milestone wasn't sure he agreed. He had already reduced the number to six.

Zanuck stood firm. "Whatever number you have, cut some more. The first two are marvelous, but after that it becomes an arty trick. Don't give the audience a chance to arrive at the same conclusion."

Because he respected Zanuck's opinion, Milestone

Facing page: *Tyne's platoon in action against an enemy halftrack. A Walk in the Sun (20th Century-Fox, 1945) is one of the few combat films in which the enemy is seldom seen; most are hidden within their machines.*

grudgingly dropped two more ballads and flew to New York to meet Spyros Skouras, the head of 20th Century-Fox.

But even before he previewed the film for the New York people, Milestone received a long telegram from Zanuck, saying that he had liked this picture so much that he had set up a special screening for the directors on the Fox lot. They unanimously agreed it was a marvelous picture but they didn't like the ballads. In the telegram, Zanuck made a point of mentioning a conversation he had had with director Ernst Lubitsch who had told him. "It's a great picture, but what the hell are the ballads doing in it?" Zanuck's final suggestion was that Milestone eliminate the ballads altogether.

Stalling for time, as he waited for the release agreement to be signed, Milestone pretended not to have received the telegram. After Skouras came through and agreed to release *A Walk in the Sun* under the 20th Century Fox logo, Milestone sent a wire to Zanuck.

"I appreciate your suggestion in regards to the ballads. Thank all the directors for their opinions and suggestions, but it's too late. I can no longer do anything because there's no more production money. We've just previewed the picture and I'm afraid it's going to go out as it is."

Although the release agreement was ratified in late April 1945, just before the German surrender in Europe, *A Walk in the Sun* did not officially premiere in New York until January 11, 1946.

The long delay probably canceled out a great deal of the film's boxoffice success. The war had been over for four months and military subjects were no longer so popular with the public. Still, the picture was a critical triumph.

The film critic for *Cue Magazine* wrote in his January review that it was "a beautifully acted, superbly photographed and directed record of a day in the life of a soldier, and an age in the life of man...."

Six months later, Los Angeles Times critic Philip K. Scheuer once more defended the film from those who still criticized its talkativeness.

"Okay," he wrote, "so the real GI's don't talk like that. But the 53 boys of this 'Texan' Division platoon do talk like that. I read them and I have seen and heard them talking like that, and what they say sounds okay to me. It is both the license and function of the artist to alter nature as much as he wishes, if by doing so he improves on it. And it is the margin of 'unnaturalness' that makes Brown's men, and now Milestone's, seem more real than real...."

The *Daily Variety* critic considered the film a "first class job of picture making," but also commented on several of the technical aspects of the film, saying "the ballads used to supplement the narration in atmosphere building have a hillbilly flavor and add little to the effectiveness of the film...."

2

The Lion Returns to War

One of the first postwar American combat films, MGM's 1949 *Battleground*, carried forward the serious attitude and perspective of Lewis Milestone's *A Walk in the Sun*. Its author, infantry veteran Robert Pirosh, won an Academy Award for his screenplay and the success of the film almost singlehandedly restarted the war film cycle after a four year lapse.

A seasoned dramatist, Pirosh wrote *Battleground* from a unique position. He had known the "battered bastards of Bastogne," the nickname given to the members of the 101st Airborne Division who defended a small town in Belgium during the Battle of the Bulge. He had slept in the same mud, picked at the same frozen K-rations, faced the same German soldiers across a stretch of snowy forest.

Pirosh had survived the war and while many men were shedding all vestiges of war memories and storing souvenirs in the sanctity of their attics, Pirosh was prepared to gamble his memories on a successful commercial film that would dramatize the untold story of the infantryman — the footslogging mud merchant.

Battleground was one of Hollywood's best kept postwar secrets. But its story begins a lot earlier, in the freezing cold of the Ardennes forest, in late December 1944.

Master Sergeant Robert Pirosh was leading a patrol near the perimeter of Bastogne. His unit, an element of the 320th Regiment, 35th Infantry Division, had been sent north from General Patton's 3rd Army to relieve the encircled 101st Airborne Division fighting for its life in the strategic highway center of Bastogne.

24

Pirosh was a veteran Hollywood screenwriter and unlike many of his coworkers who donned officer's bars only to edit film in Astoria, New York, or Culver City, he had become a combat infantryman. Before the war, he had written comedy films with his partner George Seaton. Such Films as *A Day at the Races* (with the Marx Brothers), *Up in Arms* (with Danny Kaye) and *I Married a Witch* were a far cry from wartime combat, but Pirosh kept a journal anyway, keeping track of his experiences and anecdotes.

In December 1949, during the fifth anniversary of the Battle of the Bulge, he wrote to the *New York Times* describing some of his experiences as a writer on the march:

"Some of the material for 'Battleground' came out of notes in my diary. It was not a daily diary, but my mind was always on a possible picture to be written after the war.

"For instance, there is an episode in 'Battleground' involving the Van Johnson character 'Holly' and some eggs. That came from an actual incident recorded in my wartime diary. It was my first advance to the front since I joined the outfit. One of the men found 13 eggs. 'Find me a frying pan and we'll cook 'em,' he said. Well, he never did get that frying pan, as we had to move up right away [see page 39].

"Soon after, an enemy machine gun opened up and we all hit the dirt. I noticed that he went down very slowly trying to protect the eggs. That broke the spell for me. I had to laugh. Remember, he was a seasoned veteran, I a replacement. I figured that if he could worry about eggs, then we were okay."

As his unit fought alongside the 101st Airborne in the Bulge, Pirosh continued to record his anecdotes on the backs of envelopes, Nazi propaganda leaflets, and sometimes on soft toilet tissue.

Later, while a screenwriter at Metro Goldwyn Mayer, Pirosh was able to discuss his film project with Brigadier General Anthony McAuliffe, the general whose reply of "Nuts!" to the German surrender demand at Bastogne became one of the classic moments in United States military history. McAuliffe enthusiastically approved of the project and Pirosh's plan to show only the GI viewpoint of the battle.

He agreed that it was time the public was shown a new side of war, the reactions of the average man who suddenly found him-

self in a foxhole. Later, during story conferences, McAuliffe personally annotated and approved every line of dialogue.

"This is the GI's story," he said emphatically, after removing his name from a line of dialogue. "Who cares about generals, except other generals and their families?"

The later success at MGM, however, was long in coming for Pirosh who, after World War II, first returned to RKO studios.

Like many other World War II projects then germinating in postwar Hollywood, Pirosh's story idea was ignored in favor of more lighthearted entertainment.

One morning in early 1947, he was asked to report to the new head of production at RKO, Dore Schary. Schary had known Pirosh before the war and was familiar with his experiences in the 35th Division.

Began Schary, "I think we're going to activate your Bulge project. The time has come to make a war picture. People think they won't be made for three or four years, but I think they're wrong. I want to get a shooting script ready. I already have a man in Washington doing research, and I want you to collaborate with him on the script."

Pirosh was surprised by Schary's announcement but he was not about to let the moment get the better of him.

He told Schary, "Don't even tell me who this research guy is. If you want me to write about the war, I'll do it. I don't want to collaborate with anyone, and I'll do my own research."

"All right, all right!" Schary yielded. Secretly, he was quite pleased, for he knew Pirosh was uniquely qualified to create the first postwar combat film.

Satisfied that he would be the only writer, Pirosh eagerly poured out his ideas. "I want to write purely from the viewpoint of one squad, because I was in that squad."

Today, Pirosh proudly boasts, "I avoided at least three clichés in writing the script for *Battleground*. There is no character from Brooklyn in the story. Nobody gets a letter from his wife or

---

Facing page: *The* Battleground *(MGM, 1949) team, from left: Mrs. Anthony McAuliffe, General McAuliffe, Mr. and Mrs. Dore Schary, the producer, writer Robert Pirosh, and director William Wellman.*

girl saying she has found a new love, and nobody sweats out the news of the arrival of a new born baby back home."

Given a free hand, he was able to develop the story totally around his "squad idea." Utilizing this distinct perspective, the writer disposed of high level strategy, in turn, eliminating generals and scenes at rear echelon headquarters.

"It was just what the guys knew," says Pirosh, and "they knew nothing," which echoes the thoughts of medic McWilliams in *A Walk in the Sun.*

Worried that another studio would beat them to the theaters with a rival war film, Schary designated Pirosh's story as "Prelude to Love" and kept all preproduction planning secretive. With studio authorizaiton Pirosh and an RKO still photographer went to Bastogne in April of 1947 to gather research materials for the proposed screenplay.

Pirosh was already in Europe at the time, completing a prologue sequence for a René Clair film, *Le Silence Est d'Or.* Starring Maurice Chevalier, the film was voted the best film of the year at both the Brussels and Locarno Film Festivals.

Not only was the climate in the Ardennes that spring a far cry from the snowy freezing weather that Pirosh remembered, but this time he was being chauffeured in a deluxe limousine.

Shuttling between the two and a half year old battlefield and the crossroads town of Bastogne, he recorded valuable information which, along with the new stills, would help the studio art department recreate part of the Belgian forest on the backlot.

One afternoon, during a leisurely drive through the countryside, Pirosh shouted the driver to a stop.

"It all looked strangely familiar," recalls Pirosh of a small piece of terrain he had spotted not far from Bastogne.

"I got out of the limousine and took another look across at a farm which sloped down to a dense pine forest in the distance. This was the place all right. There was the stone farmhouse and the demolished barn. Everything had been snow covered then, but there was no mistaking the scene. This was where I had stood guard, shivering under a blanket with a friend the night before we entered Harlange. And fifty yards away in a patch of woods was where our foxholes were.

"The way I ran into that patch of woods, the chauffeur

Top: *Writer Pirosh revisits Bastogne in 1947 researching his script for* Battleground *(MGM, 1949); here, he has found his old foxhole, and the remains of a K-ration.* Bottom: *Actor: Jerome Courtland (left) and John Hodiak in a scene from the film.*

must have thought I was crazy. The foxholes were still there with pine branches tossed over them, just the way we left them. Nobody had bothered to fill them in. In the hole which I had once called home, I found an empty K-ration box.

"It all came rushing back. The taste of K-rations. The sound of the 88's. The fear, the numbing cold, the exhaustion and the terrible, lonely, depression.

"And I thought of the men who had been in the other foxholes—Besser and Caswell who were captured: Beiss and Levine who were wounded; Gaumer and Gerstenkorn who went back with pneumonia; and Gettings and Butch who were killed. And then I thought of Harlange, Belgium (or was it Luxembourg?), where we went in with two platoons and came out with a couple of squads."

Such a traumatic reunion with the horror of times past, reinforced his desire to create the true "GI" picture.

"After all," he later told reporters, "what business did I have writing the epic picture of the war in Europe?"

Dore Schary, who had kept a close wrap of secrecy around the project, made an official announcement to the press on May 16, 1948, stating that *Battleground*, an original screenplay by Robert Pirosh, was to be the studio's first production since financier Howard Hughes had acquired the studio. The resulting press release confirmed that *Battleground,* a screen version of the Battle of the Bulge, was to be the biggest production of the 1948-1949 year. Schary immediately assigned producers Jesse L. Lasky and Walter MacEwen to the project and signed Robert Mitchum, Robert Ryan and Bill Williams to starring roles.

Although Howard Hughes shared Schary's enthusiasm for a new war film, he did not agree that the infantry should be the focus of a major studio production. Hughes was more interested in doing a film about air power. He also felt that Pirosh's story was too grim and that it lacked entertainment values.

Schary stood firm. Difficulties arose and clashes were narrowly averted. On the one side stood Schary, soft-spoken, creative and firmly convinced that *Battleground* was a winner. On the other side stood Hughes, new to the studio and ready to gather a new base of power. He was as firmly convinced that an infantry picture would be a disaster. Neither would budge. Finally,

A real wrecked tank on the road to Bastogne ca. *1944.* (Courtesy Western History Research Center, University of Wyoming.)

exasperated at Hughes' intransigence, Schary tendered his resignation.

The creative driving force that he was, Schary did not remain idle long. Like a highly touted college basketball prospect, Schary was immediately signed by Louis B. Mayer to head production at MGM. RKO never recovered from the loss.

With the exodus of Schary, the Pirosh script was quickly shelved. Heartbroken, Pirosh continued to work at RKO on other projects, hoping that *Battleground* could in some way be revived.

Three months later, he learned that Schary had purchased two screenplays from RKO. One a splashy costume drama entitled *Ivanhoe*, the other, to his everlasting gratitude, was *Battleground*.

That same night Schary called him. "Why get someone else to play Heifetz's fiddle when Heifetz is available?" he said, asking that Pirosh come over to MGM and rework his script.

On October 11, 1948, Schary assigned the project to producer Pandro S. Berman. But Berman left the film for a new project, and Schary took over full production chores in March 1949 on the first major studio combat film since 1945.

Although the project proceeded on schedule, there was considerable grumbling among the studio executives. Like Howard Hughes, Louis B. Mayer was skeptical and uneasy about the commercial prospects for *Battleground*. He thought it was too harrowing a story to be made so soon after the war. But to his credit, he did not try to abort the project.

"Go ahead, my boy, and make it," he told Schary, "It will teach you a lesson."

The other studio executives continally dogged Schary. They agreed with Mayer about the film's poor box office potential but, even more importantly, they felt that Schary was starting off on the wrong foot, doing a picture against the wishes of Mayer.

Despite the growing uneasiness about the film, Schary continued with the preproduction planning. Story, not topic, was the deciding factor, he maintained. The basic premise of *Battleground* was honest and sincere, dealing with the average man and his hate for war, who, despite fear, wouldn't quit.

To direct the film, Schary chose William A. Wellman, then in this artistic prime. Wellman had directed *The Story of GI Joe* for United Artists four years earlier and he approached *Battleground* with the same forcefulness and characteristic bravura.

An acknowledged expert at directing action sequence — in effect, another Lewis Milestone — Wellman was not known for his grace on the set. He had an intense dislike for ostentation.

A former member of the Lafayette Flying Corps during the First World War, Wellman brought a sensitive directorial touch to *Battleground*. It is surprising that Wellman was able to film two classic studies of the infantry, considering the comments he made in a 1970 interview.

"After all," he explained, "I was in the flying corps and we were constantly being fired on by our own infantry."

It was Ernie Pyle who changed Wellman's view on land warfare and urged him to move mountains to film *The Story of GI Joe*. Wellman had become good friends with the famous war correspondent when Pyle was on his way to the Pacific. Together they hobnobbed with W.C. Fields and Gene Fowler, got terribly drunk together and learned a great deal about each other. Pyle came to Wellman's house the night before he shipped out to the Pacific, a voyage from which he never returned. It was the sensitive view of the infantry, seen through Ernie Pyle's eyes, that Wellman brought to *The Story of GI Joe* and four years later, *Battleground*.

The crucial director/writer relationship between Wellman and Pirosh proved itself during the early story conferences as the script was rewritten and polished for the final production phase.

In April 1949, Schary promoted Pirosh to associate producer, a fact that the writer announced on the set one morning. Wellman grunted and continued to line up a scene. Eager to add new levels of realism to the film, Pirosh began to follow the crew around the studio during the preproduction phase of *Battleground*.

As he expains, "Maybe it was an obsession with me, but the uniforms never looked quite right to me. I wanted them to look as if they had been slept in for a month."

His suggestions were at first appreciated by Wellman, who agreed that fatigue and shock should be progressive, and as a result most of the picture was shot in continuity. But as production continued, Wellman's patience started to wear thin. He did not like having a writer-turned-producer peering over his shoulder, "dirtying things up." It wasn't long before Pirosh found himself barred from the set permanently.

Schary didn't feel that he could intervene, so Pirosh left the studio in bitterness. His technical advisor chores were taken over by Lt. Col. Harry Kinnard, G-3, the brains behind the defense of Bastogne.

To round out the roster of performers who would eventually fill the 18 principal speaking parts in the film, MGM acquired 20 of the original 101st Airborne paratroopers, then stationed with the 82nd Airborne Division at Fort Bragg, North Carolina.

On March 15, 1949, the 20 soldiers—11 sergeants, five corporals and four PFC's—nominated by their fellow GI's, were flown into Hollywood as a regular military unit on detached service, under the supervision of one of their regular division officers.

Producer Dore Schary (at microphone) and cast of Battleground *(MGM, 1949) greet a detachment of the 101st Airborne Division, veterans of action at Bastogne, who would work on the film. (Courtesy Western History Research Center, University of Wyoming.)*

Billeted in a motel down the street from the Culver City Studios, the soliders received $7 a day food allowance from the studio. As MGM's publicity department said, "They were generally leading the life of the Irish."

For these veterans, Bastogne had been just another hitch of patroling outside the city in the deep snow and bitter cold of the Belgian winter, bringing in occasional prisoners, dodging enemy artillery, struggling to heat their food over tiny foxhole fires and wishing they were somewhere else.

"As a matter of fact," admitted Sergeant Max Trujillo of Trinidad, Colorado, "I wouldn't know the town of Bastogne if I saw it. I spent most of the time in an old house where we had a command post a distance from Bastogne."

Casting for *Battleground* at first presented a problem. Robert Taylor, Bill Williams, Robert Ryan and Keenan Wynn all departed the project when a snag developed in contract negotiations.

To fill Taylor's shoes, Schary signed Van Johnson for the

leading part of Holly, the lover boy with a weakness for gags and girls. Johnson had a penchant for military roles, having recently completed *Command Decision*, another MGM war film, with Clark Gable.

Marshall Thompson was assigned the crucial role of Layton, the green replacement who slowly learns the true value of comradeship in Sergeant Kinny's (James Whitmore) hard pressed combat squad.

The other members of the cast included Don Taylor (an Air Force veteran), Ricardo Montalban (a newcomer from the Mexican film industry), John Hodiak, Jerome Courtland (who shone as Abner the Hillbilly), Bruce Cowling, Richard Jaeckle (the perpetual "kid" in countless war films), and Douglas Fowley (who had lost his teeth in an aircraft carrier explosion in the South Pacific).

Before principle photography began, the actors were put through a two week minicourse in basic training. Every day they fired weapons, practiced close order drill, grenade throwing, creeping and crawling. The whole group, including the 20 veterans, fell out in fatigues early in the morning, moved from one area of the MGM lot to another in 6 x 6 army trucks and smoked only during the ten minute breaks.

Stars were paired off with GI's for individual coaching, the Army's buddy system which proved so effective in wartime. Time was referred to according to the Army 24-hour system, in the daily orders posted:

0900-0950	Calisthenics
0950-1000	Ten minute break
1000-1050	Firing positions, prone, sitting, kneeling
1050-1100	Break
1100-1200	Scouting, patroling creeping, crawling
1200-1300	Lunch
1300-1350	Grenade throwing, bayonet fighting
1350-1400	Break
1400-1450	Orientation film and lecture: "How to Get

	Killed in One Easy Lesson"
1450-1500	Break
1500-1550	Truck training, mounting, dismounting, bumpy truck
1550-1600	Break
1600-1700	Script rehearsal, scenes 185, 187, 190

Pirosh's desire for dirtier uniforms were fulfilled. Laundering was strictly forbidden. As the first day of shooting commenced, Army trucks began to bounce the cast over to Backlot 3.

There were two main sets on the back lot. One was a replica of Bastogne, rebuilt from an Italian village used by United Artists in 1944 for *The Story of GI Joe* ("No wonder this town looks familiar," observed Wellman on his first day on the set).

The other set represented a pine forest in the Ardennes, reproduced on one of the MGM sound stages. A total of 528 trees were shipped to the studio from Northern Califorina. These included giant pines, identical to the Bastogne species, and nearly 300 smaller trees and shrubs to dot the terrain with such realism that one paratrooper declared that it gave him the creeps. To simulate cold, wintry Belgium, chemical snow was shipped in daily in a great mixmaster and blown about by wind machines.

True to its promise, the U.S. Army provided the necessary assortment of mobile transport and artillery. To duplicate the relief of Bastogne, a second unit camera crew was sent to the State of Washington to photograph an armored division on maneuvers.

One of Schary's difficulties was in getting the censors to approve General McAuliffe's immortal answer to the German surrender demand. The single word "nuts" had been previously barred from the screen. Schary and Wellman claimed, justly, there there wasn't a synonym for such an historic reply. They eventually won over the censors and *Battleground* achieved its final touch of historical realism.

For the special jive drill sequence opening the film, Schary secured the services of Master Sergeant Samuel Jaegers of the 94th Engineer Construction Battalion at Fort Belvoir, Virginia. Jaegers, a Southern university graduate, was one of the originators of "jive," a stepped-up version of regulation close order drill, which served to brighten up the routine aspects of essential training methods.

"Bombshell ... March! ... To the Rear ... Freeze! and "T-Formation ... Hit it!" were typical unorthodox commands that became instantly popular with black troops and others.

Along with "jive" came the famous "Jody Chant," a song created to avoid the repetitious "left, right, left" of the marching cadence. Jody, of course, was the mythical female, who remained at home at attend to financial and romantic matters, while her boy friend or husband went off to war.

You had a good home   Sound off!
But you left   One, two.
You're right!
                                         Sound off!
Jody was there   Three, four,
When you left
You're right!   Cadence count!
                                         One, two, three, four —
Your baby was there   One, two,
When you left   Three, four.
You're right!

Each company would compose its own verse, some of which were quite obscene. In preparing the script, Pirosh had been guided by propriety, not memory.

Having completed its production phase routinely on June 3, 1949, *Battleground* went through its editing, scoring and sound effects phases before opening at the Astor Theater in New York and then simultaneously at the Metro Theater in Antwerp, Belgium, the Forum Theater in Liège and the General Patton Theater in Bastogne. The film arrived in Los Angeles for a major premiere on December 1, 1949.

As predicted by Dore Schary, *Battleground* became the big boxoffice champ of 1949. On December 2, Hollywood columnist and critic Louella Parsons could not help but agree. She wrote, "*Battleground* is MGM's big picture of the year. No greater compliment could be given the film than to say that it has been given 100% approval by all the men who actually fought at Bastogne,

Top: *Jarvis (John Hodiak) and Holly (Van Johnson) mourn the loss of a friend.*
Bottom: *The kid grows up: Holly greets Layton (Marshall Thompson, standing)
and actress Michelle Montau, the only female in* Battleground *(MGM, 1949).*

Top: *"Kip" (Douglas Fowley, left) listens to "Pop" (George Murphy) explain his inability to report to the rear for transfer stateside — Bastogne is surrounded.* Bottom: *Writer Pirosh's eggs incident is brought to life on-screen: Richard Jaeckle, left, and Van Johnson.* — Battleground *(MGM, 1949).*

men who usually look down their noses at war pictures as glorified movie ideas...."

The critic for *Look* magazine saw *Battleground*, "as 'The Big Parade' of World War II," while the critic for the daily *Variety*, called it "a paean, but minus the phony heroics usually associated with such exploits."

Continued the *Variety* critic, "This dogface is the one Ernie Pyle and Bill Mauldin came to know so well. A member of the kind of platoon that gets called up every time there is a dirty detail, he finds himself on a cold day in December 1944 in another mangy, strangely named town—Bastogny, he thinks it's pronounced."

Slogging through mud with grim determination, and ignoring the constant smell of death around them, Sergeant Kinny's soldiers had survived. Indicative of their never failing spirit is the film's final scene. A poignant climax, created by a writer who was looking backwards, and still retained that "direct from the headlines" perspective.

Kinny's men are sitting by the side of a Belgian road, perparing to march rearward. Their war is over. As they watch the reinforcements pass by in their polished tanks and immaculate uniforms, the sun begins to shine, and there is relief in the air.

Shouting an emphatic "good luck" to a passing tank crew, Kinny orders his squad to its feet. Their clothes are fifthy, their beards are shaggy, and they are bone-tired. It appears that they are headed back to the front, but Kinny, playing out the drama, orders them "about face" and they march sullenly to the rear.

They sluff along wearily, oblivious to their surroundings. The road is empty and their minds dwell on the luxuries of a bed and a warm shower.

Holly taps Kinny on the shoulder and points to a column of new recruits marching their way. The tattered Sergeant brushes off his uniform, throws away his cigar and orders his shattered unit to look sharp. A cue is whispered and they begin the immortal Jody chant, slowly at first, and then, as they pick up the rhythm, they shout it out. The end titles appear as the MGM orchestra joins in.

Facing page: *On an MGM soundstage that looks incredibly like Ardennes Forest of winter 1944, a group of airborne troopers greet a German surrender detachment.* —Battleground *(MGM, 1949).*

And this type of ending had a distinct effect on the postwar audiences. People emerged from the theater remembering the humanity of Pirosh's soldiers, not their victory over the Germans in the Bulge. They vividly remembered the platoon's spirit, which had allowed them to complete that last mission, which had brought them one more step closer to home.

3

A Fox's Gamble

For showman Darryl Francis Zanuck and 20th Century-Fox Film Corporation, the fall of 1960 was a crucial period.

One of Hollywood's all-time most successful producers and studio executives, Zanuck had turned independent in 1956 and in the space of four short years, turned a series of worthwhile film properties into costly, overblown productions, each one a major disappointment at the boxoffice. These less than successful 20th Century-Fox releases included *The Sun Also Rises* (1957), *The Roots of Heaven* (1958), and *Crack in the Mirror* (1960).

Earlier, in 1952, the seeds of further disintegration were sown with the appearance of Bella Wegier or Bella Darvi, as she was billed in another series of costly duds (*Hell and High Water, The Racers,* and *The Egyptian*). Zanuck's infatuation with this French girl who couldn't act not only clouded his film sense but it brought about the dissolution of his 30 year marriage to Virginia Zanuck (incidentally, Bella Darvi's last name is composed of the first parts of the names Darryl and Virginia).

Throughout the period, 20th Century-Fox was in increasingly desperate financial straits. Its investments in Zanuck's personal productions were proving painfully unprofitable and the studio was about to enter the *Cleopatra* era, a period of even further financial decline and creative stagnation.

Zanuck left the studio in 1956, surrendering production chores to Buddy Adler, formerly of Columbia Pictures, who had produced the very successful *From Here to Eternity*. Adler worked hard to reorganize the unwieldy studio structure and return it to solvency, but when he died suddenly four years later, the task was left unfinished.

43

The Parachute drop on Ste. Mère Église. — The Longest Day *(20th Century-Fox, 1962).*

Zanuck refused to stay down, nor let the studio that had always been his home crumble into receivership. In 1960 he returned to produce *The Longest Day*, the most important film he would ever create.

Like a ruptured artery, the spiraling costs on *Cleopatra* would eventually drain the studio's life blood. It was up to Zanuck to replenish the loss with the infusion of boxoffice plasma.

Zanuck saw *The Longest Day* as the chance of a lifetime. He was right. And his timing proved perfect. The film eventually became a huge success and saved 20th Century-Fox from financial ruin.

In many ways the production of this blockbuster recreation of the June 6, 1944, Normandy invasion equaled the complexity of the original historical event. The undertaking eventually cost more money, took up more screen time, featured more directors and international stars, and included more technical assistance than any other American combat film ever conceived to that time. But it was worth every penny and every minute and to this day it represents the perfect image of what D.W. Griffith originally viewed as a history lesson on film.

Although later critics attacked the film as lacking serious comment on the true cost of D-Day, *The Longest Day* was lauded by others for its documentary style, the accuracy of its historical framework, and its professional, fast moving story telling.

On the 25th anniversary of D-Day, in June of 1969, Darryl F. Zanuck revisited the wind swept beaches near the Norman town of Colleville and reminisced.

"This was it," he mused. "Bloody Omaha. When I announced that I was going to produce *The Longest Day,* many people asked me why? I had my reasons. I served in World War I when I was 14 years old. I also served in World War II as a colonel in France and North Africa. It was then that I first heard the story of *The Longest Day.*

"The incredible story of D-Day and the invasion of Nazi occupied Europe fascinated me. It was unquestionably the most hazardous undertaking in military history, and it was a story that I felt had to be told.

"If people could see the brutality and inhumanity of war. I reasoned they would be filled will such revulsion that they would never permit their leaders to send them back to the battlefield. I was wrong. In spite of the worldwide success of *The Longest Day*, in spite of the fact that more people saw it than any other black and white film in history, wars in various forms continue to this day."

Another man also stood on the beach reminiscing with Darryl Zanuck. Military historian Cornelius Ryan had been a war correspondent for the *London Daily Express* assigned to cover the Normandy landings when the Allies hit the beach on June 6, 1944. For all his experience and expertise, Ryan still found it difficult to write meaningfully about the invasion.

He later wrote, "Out of the dawn, a million men plowed ashore through the surf, flags flying and marched on Berlin. Ridiculous. On that gray and misty morning, fewer than 9,000 men landed on a fifty mile stretch in the first wave. They came in a thin straggly line of landing craft.

"It seemed more like a Madison Avenue affair. The organization was fantastic. Five thousand ships, fifteen thousand planes, hundreds of correspondents...

"You couldn't help asking yourself, 'What's that soldier thinking about? Had anyone considered the villagers on the coast? What did the Free French feel as they fired on their homeland...?' "

Ryan felt totally inadequate to report the historical event. He felt there was no way to tell the whole story without getting inside the men who were living it.

"I knew I had to get this down on paper in an informed way. I had to be able to say, '*This* is the way it was!' If I had been a soldier, I might not have been interested in finding out why, why it was the way it was. But I was just young enough to be angry with myself for not knowing ... not understanding. I was determined to find out everything I could, the stupid things, the mad things, the courageous things. I had to know."

But D-Day ended and Ryan left to join General Patton's 3rd Army. And after the war in Europe ended, he was ordered to the Far East.

The idea for a book on D-Day did not return to him until 1949 when a group of the original correspondents returned to Normandy for the fifth anniversary of D-Day.

Ryan recalled, "I walked along the beach and saw the flotsam and jetsam of war still cluttering the area, burned out vehicles, weapons... I watched as a fisherman dragged a howitzer out of the sea with his net. A skeleton, helmet still in place, protecting the empty skull, was tangled up somehow with the cannon's wheels. Who was he? Nobody, nobody anywhere, knew. Nobody knew which men had landed on D-Day in the first wave. What an appalling thing.

"And yet, who was there to keep track? Who possibly had the time to record the happenings? Not the participants. It was then that I began to think seriously about writing a book about the happenings of Normandy on that fateful day."

At that time, Ryan was working for *Colliers* magazine, but he could not interest his employer, or any other magazine, in financing his proposed project. He started anyway, sustaining himself with his own money. He began searching for records, for people. He ran advertisements: "Where were you on June 6, 1944? Contact me if you took part in D-Day.'

"I began writing to survivors. I sent out 6,000 questionnaires. Two thousand answered. Out of the two thousand came 700 interviews. There were some 240 books written on D-Day. I read them all."

In 1956, Colliers went bankrupt. Ryan was about $20,000 in debt, money he had borrowed to cover his travel, correspondence and translation expenses.

"My wife Kathryn was then an editor at *House and Home,* and we talked it over and decided that I should devote full time to the book. I began writing in earnest, and when I took the first pages of the book to Simon & Schuster, they gave me an advance of $7,500.

"I finished *The Longest Day* three years later. Kathryn and I had worked seven days a week with absolutely no time off for at least three or four years. Even though I finally received financial and research help from *Reader's Digest,* by the time we finished, we were still about $60,000 in debt.

"I turned the manuscript in and walked directly over to the *Digest* to ask for an assignment. Then I went home and Kathryn and I stared at each other. Suddenly, we didn't know what to do with ourselves."

Reader's Digest condensed Ryan's book and *The Longest*

Day first appeared in the spring of 1959. One month later, Simon & Schuster published the hard cover version.

It became a landmark work of nonfiction, establishing Ryan as one of the country's top military historians. Ryan used this reputation to go on and write two more epic war stories, *The Last Battle* (about the battle for Berlin in the final days of the European War) and *A Bridge Too Far* (a fascinating study of the tragic Market Garden airborne landings in Holland in 1944, which became a huge film production in 1977, directed by Richard Attenborough of *The Great Escape* fame).

French film producer Raoul J. Levy, the man who discovered curvaceous French sex symbol Brigitte Bardot, took an option on Ryan's novel, and on March 23, 1960, he closed a deal with Simon & Schuster to acquire the complete rights. Ryan was to receive $100,000 for the film rights, plus another $35,000 to write the screenplay.

Within a week, Levy contacted several major American producing companies, including Columbia Pictures, which had first refusal on all Levy projects, in an attempt to set up a financing/distribution deal.

Levy envisioned *The Longest Day* as a true blockbuster that would cost at least six milion dollars to make. He also announced his intention to seek military cooperation from Britain, France, Germany and the United States. He predicted that filming would begin in the spring of 1961.

While Ryan was beginning what was to be a very long screenplay, Levy was busy filming *La Vérité* and Mlle Bardot. When that project was finished, Levy began arrangements for *The Longest Day*. Failing to secure an American production company, he set up a deal with Associated British Picture Corporation, and then flew to Washington, D.C., to confer with members of the Defense Department.

At Dulles International Airport, he informed reporters that Englishman Michael Anderson had been signed as director, with Erwin Hillier, who had been the cinematographer on *The Dam Busters*, handling the photography.

In an interview with the daily *Variety,* Levy revealed that Ryan had been hired to write the script, and "although the cast is not as yet set ... there will be around 300 speaking parts in the film, and of these about fifty will be of star caliber American, British, French and German performers. Most of the top French actors we've contacted are eager to be in the film."

His plans were to get production rolling by March 1961; interiors would be done at Elstree Studios outside London; other shooting would be on the English coast and in France. To handle the broad sweep of the film, he envisioned as many as twenty camera crews working on the production at once. He further predicted that *The Longest Day* would be the first contemporary epic.

Levy's plans, however, came to an abrupt and unexpected halt when the executives of Associated British Pictures informed him that they were unable to come up with the projected $6 million budget.

Like Samuel Bronston, who had run into the same problem some 16 years earlier while attempting to finance *A Walk the Sun*, Levy learned the hard way that independent producers, even successful ones, ran into critical snares when attempting to bankroll a costly picture.

No sooner was Levy shot down by the British, than Zanuck stepped in to revive the project. He had been filming *The Big Gamble* with Stephen Boyd and Juliette Greco, on Africa's Ivory Coast, when Ryan's book had been published. When Levy grabbed a first option, Zanuck waited to see what he would do with the project. When it fell through, he stepped in and purchased Levy's option.

Although somewhat wary about putting up some large sums of money for a war picture, the Fox executives were even more anxious to back a winner that could lift the studio out of the deepening red. Production bills on *Cleopatra* were arriving from Italy in horrendous numbers and amounts. Filming had gone from bad in London to worse in Rome.

One of the basic mistakes had been in picking rainy England for the shooting of a sunny Egyptian story, and the climactic error was compounded by two more strokes of bad fortune. Actress Elizabeth Taylor fell in love with her costar Richard Burton, and then she contracted pneumonia in London, both of which events were almost fatal, one to the studio and the other to the new Queen of the Nile.

Another two and half million dollars trickled down the

drain when Joseph Mankiewicz was hired to write at night and direct by day an unbelievable off the cuff operation that by 1962 had pyramided production costs to over $35 million.

In an effort to save the studio from ruin, the Fox executives decided that if Zanuck could indeed acquire *The Longest Day*, they would gamble the studio's last financial reserves on the project.

Elmo Williams, a 20th Century-Fox second unit director and the future producer of *Tora! Tora! Tora!*, had reinforced Zanuck's belief in the potential of the film, as well as its logistical demands.

"It's going to take a lot of guts to make this picture," he told Zanuck pointedly. Williams laid out in cold figures the mountain of equipment that would be required, the manpower and directorial skill it would take to do the job well, and the pressure of finding a huge workable cast of international players.

Zanuck understood the complexities. He felt, as did Levy, that to do justice to the tremendous scope of the story, shooting would have to be done on authentic location sites whenever possible. And, despite the obvious cost, only great stars of international renown would be cast.

On December 2, 1960, Zanuck purchased the film rights to Ryan's novel from Levy for $175,000. The large sum included the writer's compensation for a new screenplay.

In a news conference, it was Zanuck's turn to announce his plans. The showman he was, he did not spare words.

"I feel that it will probably be the most ambitious undertaking since *Gone with the Wind* and *Birth of a Nation*. What will it cost? God knows! I don't know. Certainly millions. Either I will go broke, or make the greatest picture ever. I believe that from a patriotic standpoint, we can get stars to fill all of the major roles."

Zanuck emphasized that the production would not "be a war picture as such" but rather "the story of the little people, of the underground, of the civilians who were there, of the unknown men who made the first assault, of the general confusion." He concluded, "My picture will hate the institution of war, but be fair about it."

With Elmo Williams taking charge of the technical aspects of the battle sequences, and Ryan working on the new script,

Zanuck sent producer Frank McCarthy first to Washington, D.C., and then to Europe to secure the military cooperation vital to the success of the film.

McCarthy, a brigadier general during World War II and aide to Chief of Staff General Marshall, recalls his important assignment this way: "General Lauris Norstad was then commander of the NATO forces and I went to him after getting script approval from Washington. Norstad promised us complete cooperation and about 700 special forces troops. These soldiers were stationed far from the border and they were selected on the theory that should there be any trouble with the Russians in Berlin, they could be sent to the capital from Normandy just as readily as they could from their bases in Southern Germany."

To better coordinate the preproduction phase of *The Longest Day* Zanuck moved an army of secretaries, translators, researchers, and agents to the Rue de Bac, in Paris. Ryan continued the screenplay in his hotel room at the Prince de Galles Hotel, which he had converted into an office.

Originally, it had been decided to have Williams coordinate and direct each battle scene in the film but Zanuck soon realized that with seven major battle segments, it would be more practical to have multiple camera crews, filming scenes simultaneously on the different locations.

One of the assistant directors subsequently hired to film these sequences was Gerd Oswald, who had directed action sequences on two previous 20th Century-Fox war films, *Decision Before Dawn* and *The Desert Fox*.

Recalled Oswald, "Zanuck's notion at the time was, I believe, to hire a group of directors who are known in the movie industry as 'lightweights.' He avoided strong, well-established directors who could possibly stray from Darryl's law. Zanuck wanted to run the whole show and he decided to hire only those directors he felt he could control and who would not question his decisions."

In addition to Oswald, Zanuck's staff of directors would include Andrew "Bundy" Marton, Ken Annakin, and Bernhard Wicki. And later in the film, during the interiors at the Boulogne Studios in Paris, Zanuck directed a great part of the film on his own, a first in his career.

Teaming with Cornelius Ryan, Elmo Williams laid out eight major battle sequences, the largest number ever to appear in a major studio combat film. The sequences covered the Omaha Beach landing, the Utah Beach landing, the Ranger assault on Pointe du Hoc, the French commando attack on Ouistreham, the airborne landing in Ste. Mère Église, the glider assault on the Orne River bridge and the destruction of the Colleville strongpoint.

Because of the film's length, the Colleville segment ended up on the cutting room floor, much to William's dismay.

Says Williams, "I didn't mind giving up any other battle sequence, except that one. It would have been the greatest ever seen on the screen, but it would have taken up twenty minutes of screen time.

"We had a group of German S.S. troops holed up in a blockhouse behind the American invasion beach, near the town of Colleville. When the Americans go ashore they drive the Germans back, and many of the beach defenders also wind up in the crowded blockhouse. These were the ordinary Wehrmacht troops, and they wanted to give up, but the S.S. fanatics wouldn't let them. They ended up forcing the Wehrmacht to fight at gunpoint. They actually had machine guns inside the blockhouse pointed at their own men, and they held out for quite a long time because their strongpoint was well fortified. Finally, after naval bombardment proved ineffective, the Army brought up flamethrowers and fired into the airvents on top of the bunker. They kept firing until all of the oxygen inside the blockhouse was burned off.

"It was an unusual sequence because the S.S. officers knew what was going on outside, and they tried to get the soldiers to conserve their air. They were actually counting when the soldiers could breathe. It was really eerie, but we had to take it out of the picture because we already had close to a four hour film, which was much too long."

Regarding the logistics for filming these ambitious battle sequences, Zanuck wrote a letter to Lord Mountbatten, stating, "I believe I have a tougher job than Ike had on D-Day. At least he had the equipment. I have to find it, rebuild it and transport it to Normandy."

Thus began one of the greatest scavenger hunts in war film history. For the Orne River glider assault, Zanuck ordered two

The Germans discover one of the Rupert decoys. — The Longest Day *(20th Century-Fox, 1962).*

Horsa gliders from a British piano company, the same firm that had constructed the gliders during wartime. For the film's strafing sequences, Zanuck needed functioning World War II Spitfires and Messerschmitts, which were practically nonexistant. Fortunately, Williams found three Spitfires serving with the Belgian Air Force and two Messerschmitts in Spain, attached to General Franco's small air squadron.

At several locations along the Normandy Coast, work gangs were rebuilding and refurbishing many of the surviving Nazi fortifications, once part of Hitler's so-called *Festung Europa* (Fortess Europe). Milk cans once used by the Germans as mines but later dug up and reused by the French for their original purpose, were bought by Zanuck and once more restored, this time as dummy explosives.

To provide one of the film's lighter moments, Zanuck acquired the designs for the Rupert decoy. Dropped from a plane behind the Normandy coast in the dark morning hours of D-Day, Rupert engaged large groups of German soldiers and fought pitched battles with them amid the confusion of the hedgerow country. It was only after the Germans had surrounded the enemy and had blasted him to shreds that they discovered the Allied trick. Rupert was but a rubber dummy covered with fire crackers. There were thousands of Ruperts and they served twin purposes. Not only did they draw off and confuse the Germans, but they lulled them into the belief that reported paratroop landings were nothing more than purposeful diversions from the real invasion which was expected to the north, at the Pas de Calais.

The amount of ammunition needed to supply the two movie armies was one of Zanuck's biggest headaches. Over 600,000 rounds of blank ammunition had to be hand manufactured in the United States, Great Britain, Germany, Holland, and Norway.

One Belgian gunsmith was commissioned to produce a supply of handmade blanks for a German antiaircraft gun at ten dollars a shell.

Zanuck complained, "That S.O.B. wanted screen credit—ammunition by so and so. We eventually shot off about $8,000 worth in one night outside Ste. Mère Église."

France's Secret Army Organization, which was at the peak of its terrorist activity, became a complicating factor while The Longest Day was being filmed. The French government frequently voiced its nervousness over Zanuck's vast cache of arms and ammunition. As a security precaution, most of the automatic small arms were kept under police guard at all times, as were the Frenchmen cast in the various German roles in the film.

The French memory was long and the German uniforms were still a hated and feared ensemble in France. When a swastika was flown over the ancient castle of Chantilly near Paris (simulating German headquarters at La Roche Guyon), a riot was nearly caused.

Besides the 700 special forces troops promised by the NATO command, Britain, through Lord Mountbatten, pledged a fleet of 66 ships of World War II vintage and 150 men from the East Anglia and Green Jackets brigades. France, despite pressing problems in Algeria, provided over two thousand men. West Germany could muster no soldiers, but the civilian government did promise all the World War II material it could find, along with valuable technical assistance.

I negotiated for nearly eight months," recalled Zanuck in a 1962 article in *Life* magazine. "I needed a great deal of material for a period of almost a year. In return, I agreed that each of the participating governments could review the finished film and censor anything that might appear to be offensive."

Along the Normandy coast, Zanuck's corps of engineers continued to pave the way for the production crews, clearing out any vintage mines and burning off the overgrown shrubbery to reveal the pockmarked terrain of D-Day Normandy.

During the clearing operation, they unearthed a British tank in the sands where it had been buried for 17 years. With a little help from the makeup department, it was restored to serviceable condition joining Zanuck's small, but capable, tank corps.

Uniforms for the Allies were no problem. The regular troops were already outfitted in battle dress that needed few alterations to bring them back to 1944 standards.

British and U.S. military depots were amply stocked with uniforms for the additional civilian extras who masqueraded as soldiers. But the German uniforms had to be especially tailored. The West German Army had previously destroyed all reminders of Nazi days. Since Chancellor Konrad Adenauer, alone among Zanuck's "allies," could not spare any genuine soldiers for the production, the German soldiers, themselves, presented another special problem.

The solution became an elite corps of 60 French and German actors who were recruited in Paris and packed off to basic training near Versailles for a one month course in the Nazi manual of arms and the goosestep, under the supervision of former Wehrmacht paratrooper Johnny Jendrich.

How much sensitivity remained in Normandy in 1961 was vividly demonstrated at Ste. Mère Église. The first night of work, Jendrich thought it would be amusing to have his little "army" march into the town smartly, heavy boots hitting the cobblestones in well-remembered and fearfully recalled rhythm. The large French crowd that had gathered to watch the filming burst into violent anger, stones started flying and the loudspeaker echoed across the angry mob to explain that these were movie extras and not German storm troopers.

Jendrich's unit of 60 men later proved to be the workhorses of the film. They were defeated at the Orne River bridge, overrun at Omaha Beach, surrounded at Ouistreham, ambushed by the French underground, strafed by Spitfires, and surprised by the Rangers at Pointe du Hoc.

The equipment continued to pour into Zanuck's forward base of operations in Caen, Normandy. A 20mm Wehrmacht cannon was found in England. It had been captured at Dieppe during the war. Several 50mm antiaircraft guns used by the Germans were found in bunkers on the Il de Rey near La Rochelle. A British piat gun, which resembled the American bazooka, was loaned from a London museum, and a German Maxim heavy machine gun was located in Paris and sent to Caen with hundreds of rifles and sub-machine guns.

Special props, such as Rommel's ceremonial baton, had to be manufactured. It was copied from a photograph supplied by Mrs. Rommel who was later credited as a technical advisor on the film.

Two items, prop master Sam Gordon was unable to find. One was the Indian type of machete knives which the Free French commandos carried during the invasion. They had obtained the long bladed weapons while training in India. The other was a simple item: a 48 star American flag. This had to be specially created.

Throughout the Spring of 1961, Darryl F. Zanuck, a movie Eisenhower with a perpetual cigar shoved between his teeth, organized his "armada." Williams' original plan had called for all of the actual invasion scenes to be filmed on the actual locations. But practicality, a strained budget, and the French tourist season forced a change in those carefully laid plans.

Zanuck considered transferring Sword Beach, where the main British forces landed, to the other side of the English Channel where there would be a ready supply of English natives on hand to fill the ranks of the movie army. A level beach, similar to the broad sandy plain characteristic of Sword was discovered, but production plans were shelved when a group of irate bird enthusiasts warned the producer that a sanctuary was too near the beaches.

Finding Lord Mountbatten's naval flotilla useless because of its great fuel bill, a cost that Her Majesty's Navy was not going to foot, Zanuck soon found himself in drastic need of a naval flotilla and an invasion beach free of tourists and rare pheasants.

The battle action required almost two miles of uninhabited beach to film with the required sweep. This was not going to be one of those closeup sequences showing two dozen Marines scrambling ashore at Santa Monica. It would be the real thing, with at least a thousand extras in dozens of landing craft sweeping into a beach fortified with actual defenses. Closeups would be reshot later, in the off season, on their original Normandy sites but Zanuck could not afford to keep his second unit crews idle during the entire summer while he filmed indoors at the Boulogne Studios in Paris. He needed beaches right away.

In May 1961, the producer was able to train his cameras on a major British-staged paratroop drop on the island of Cyprus, but landing beaches still remained elusive.

While Zanuck and his staff were scouting equipment and locations, the author turned screenwriter was in Paris completing the script. On May 15, Zanuck arrived to find Ryan and the fattest screenplay he had even seen.

Says Zanuck, "He had things completely out of proportion, twenty-six pages for something that should take three lines and three lines for something that should have taken twenty-six pages. It was a painstaking thing. Rewriting, and rewriting, and rewriting and more rewriting." Working in each other's pockets (the uneasy relationship between writer and producer would later explode), the pair eventually finished the script.

To celebrate that occasion, Frank McCarthy brought good news from Washington. The U.S. Sixth Fleet was planning major amphibious maneuvers with the Marine complement and McCarthy reported that photographic coverage could be arranged. Leaving Ken Annakin and Bernard Wicki behind to organize the construction of the interiors at the Boulogne Studios, Zanuck, Williams, Oswald, Marton and a crew of 165 left Paris for Naples, Italy. Their final destination: the broiling sands of Saleccia Beach in Northern Corsica.

Permission had been granted to fortify the Corsican beach so that it would resemble Omaha Beach in 1944. Steel obstacles were constructed along a two-mile stretch and special effects charges were buried in the water and sand. Machine gun simulators, firing tiny ballbearings, were stationed to cover the surf.

Problems continued. The subtropical beach was obviously not the Channel coast and the wedgewood skies of Corsica bore no resemblance to the brooding clouds over Normandy. However, since the Marines were going to land over a two-day period, Zanuck and his directors were able to work something out. Early each morning, before the Marines stormed ashore, the movie crew hosed down the beaches to make them look dark as the Norman shore. The billowing smoke of burning tires, combined with several varieties of camera filters, turned the sky to an acceptable grey.

Zanuck's personal intelligence corps warned him that a nudist colony, just two miles inland from the beach, posed a potential hazard. It was arranged, therefore for the local authorities to post signs warning the nudists not to go near the water during the landings.

During the voyage from Naples to Saleccia, Zanuck had kept his unit busy photgraphing the transports en route, lecturing the troops and arranging the proposed camera coverage with the Admiral in charge.

Gerd Oswald discusses the ship board routine: "Our base of operations was in the flagship. Every night, Elmo, Bundy and I would go to a different ship and try to explain to the Marines what we were filming. Unfortunately, with a vast number of people like this (1600 Marines) we were unable to give personal directions. We couldn't say 'you drop dead here, you get hit by a bullet in the leg, and you do this.' We had to trust them.

"We tried to make the Marines realize that a couple of them had to 'die' and a couple of them had to be 'wounded.' Some of the guys told us that the Marines always made it. 'Yes,' we replied, 'but we're making a movie, not a commercial!'"

At the end of the voyage, the Sixth Fleet entered French waters and rendezvoused with a squadron of French ships that would act as a liaison during the Corsican maneuvers.

With the refreshing taste of wine and the aroma of fresh baked bread (a pleasant change after the U.S. Navy diet of Coca Cola and hash), Zanuck prepared his unit for disembarkation.

Pleased with the two-mile stretch of fortified beach constructed by his art directors, he began to place his camera crews with all of the precision of a defending field marshal.

With the combined fleet of 22 ships in the background representing the D-Day armada (which in reality had closer to 5,000 ships), everything was ready for the Marines. Shortly before H-Hour, however Zanuck noticed an aircraft carrier riding at anchor near the Marine transports. Since there were no carriers present in the channel on D-Day, Zanuck went right to the Admiral of the fleet with a request.

"Can you hide it? he asked.

"No, we can't hide it," was the answer, "if we did how could we have exercises?"

It was a problem, but there was no time to lose. Measuring the fleet, Zanuck quickly sat down and with Williams figured that if the carrier kept to the right two thousands yards, the camera crews could stil photograph the entire fleet. The calculation worked and Saleccia Beach received its last touch of realism.

At 2 p.m. on June 21, 1961, the first wave of assault boats, carrying the men of the 3rd Marine Battalion (reinforced) arrived at the beach. Ramps dropped down and the attackers came wading through the deep water wearing 1944 type leggings and net covered helmets.

Since most of the Marines were seasick (a gale wind was blowing that day) they could hardly wait to get off the landing craft and instead of coming up smiling (which was one of Zanuck's worries) they looked as grim as though they were entering actual combat.

Zanuck's crew was aided by the French LST *Argens* which ferried in supplies. Oswald summed up the Corsica maneuvers:

"We didn't really know what the men would do. I was supervising three cameras and whenever I saw something interesting, I told my crew to shoot it. We just shot on a one take deal. Eventually, in the cutting room, the best scenes were all put together."

While cameras were recording invasions and paratroop drops in documentary fashion, a great international cast was being assembled.

Oddly enough, the first people hired were a group of young American rock and roll singers. Relates Williams, "Darryl and I

were having lunch at Fouquettes in Paris when an agent friend came over and said, 'Hey, I hear you're going to make this film, why don't you let me give you a hell of bargain with some names.' So he told us about these singers. Darryl asked me what I thought, so I said, honestly, that 'you can't tell one guy from another when he's wearing a helmet, so why not?' Zanuck said okay, and they were the first actors signed."

One month later, Fabian, Tommy Sands, and Paul Anka, all popular American teen idols, were "processed" in Paris and shipped to Andrew Marton's unit at Pointe du Hoc. Their mission: don Ranger outfits and scale the 80-foot cliffs in four minutes.

Vivacious redhead Irina Demich became one of only three women in *The Longest Day*. Zanuck discovered her at a cocktail party in Paris and immediately signed her for the part of Janine Boitard, the French resistance worker, who in real life saved 68 Allied flyers from the Germans. In the off-camera Parisian social scene, Irina replaced Juliette Greco as Zanuck's companion.

In all, Zanuck spent over $2 million on major talent casting, a figure that did not include extras. After the rock and roll singers were signed on, it was superstar John Wayne who opened the floodgates of talent. When William Holden left the picture, the Duke took over the key part of Lt. Col. Benjamin Vandervoort, the 82nd Airborne officer whose broken ankle did not prevent him from leading his men into Ste. Mère Église on D-Day.

After Wayne signed, other major American actors soon followed. They included Robert Mitchum, Rod Steiger, Jeffrey Hunter, Eddie Albert, Henry Fonda, Robert Ryan, Red Buttons, Robert Wagner, George Segal, Edmond O'Brien and Tom Tryon. In all there were 28 American actors portraying everyone from Ike on down. Henry Grace, an MGM set designer, won the coveted role of Eisenhower. It was his acting debut.

Leading the British cast, which featured 15 stars, was Richard Burton, who, along with Roddy McDowell, was shuttling back and forth between *Cleopatra* and *The Longest Day*.

For one English part, Zanuck had to choose between Sean Connery, Patrick McGoohan and John Gregson. It was Connery

---

Facing page: *The U.S. Army hits the beach at Omaha, D-Day: in reality, these are U.S. Marines on maneuvers and the beach is on Corsica.* — The Longest Day *(20th Century-Fox, 1962).*

Top: *Between takes, John Wayne (left) plays chess (with a wrongly positioned board) with singer Paul Anka.* Bottom: *Producer Darryl Zanuck with ever-present cigar listens to actor Robert Wagner's ideas on a scene.* — The Longest Day *(20th Century-Fox, 1962).*

who first approached Zanuck about the part of an outspoken British private fighting on Sword Beach. But, there was a conflict. The young Scot had a commitment with United Artists for a film in Jamaica which would begin shooting in January 1962. Through some heavy negotiating, Connery was able to squeeze into *The Longest Day*, while still honoring his commitments in Jamaica. The latter film turned out to be *Dr. No*, the first James Bond film.

The 24 French and German actors completed the star-studded cast that ranks as the largest in motion picture history. Frank McCarthy describes the methods used to employ the massive group of top performers:

"Although Ryan's finished screenplay was very much like his book, certain liberties were taken to accommodate the large cast. For example, if a character was very strong in a scene in the first ten minutes of the film, Ryan would find a way to lace him in somewhere else for a couple of minutes, so that you had some hemstitching throughout the picture. You would see a little bit of Richard Todd and then you wouldn't see him and then you would see him a little more. This was done with many of the actors."

To add crucial factors of realism to the characterizations, as well as the the action, Zanuck received a great deal of advice and assistance from a group of D-Day participants.

Lord Mountbatten led a British advisory team that included the Earl of Lovat and Major John Howard. Zanuck, who had served with Mountbatten during World War II was still apprehensive about going to the English for substantial help.

"I found," he recalled, "a slightly hostile feeling, based on the fact that they thought this was another one of those American movies which showed how the Americans won the war. They wanted to be sure I wasn't interested in making it a one-man show. I told them what I was planning and that realistically, I had to have their cooperation."

Lord Lovat eventually coached actor Peter Lawford in the role of the colorful British commando leader who, dressed in a knit sweater, led his men onto Sword Beach. Howard advised actor Richard Todd in the role of the leader of a small band of glider infantry whose surprise assault on the Orne River bridge advanced the Allied cause by weeks. Tood, himself, was no stranger to D-Day Normandy. A paratroops veteran, he had jumped a few miles from the bridge on invasion day.

Top: *The real Earl of Lovat discusses the war with the movie Lord Lovat (Peter Lawford). Many veterans cooperated to give the film authenticity.* Bottom: *Lawford links his command with that of Major John Howard (Richard Todd, center), whose small force of glider-borne infantry holds the Orne River bridge.* — The Longest Day *(20th Century-Fox, 1962).*

Director Bernhard Wicki (left) discusses a scene with actor Werner Hinz, playing Field Marshal Erwin Rommel. Man at center not identified. — The Longest Day *(20th Century-Fox, 1962).*

Through General Norstad of NATO, Zanuck contacted veterans on the German side as well. Senior among these was Vice Admiral Friedrich Ruge, retiring commander-in-chief of the German Navy. Ruge, Rommel's naval aide during D-Day, in turn, found General Gunther Blumentritt (Field Marshal Von Rundstedt's chief of staff), Lt. Gen. Max Pemsel (the 7th Army chief of staff) and Major Werner Pluskat (an officer of the 352nd Division, and one of the first German officers to view the approaching Allied armada).

With the valuable assistance of these officers, actors Curt Jurgens (Blumentritt), Wolfgang Preiss (Pemsel), and Hans Christian Blech (Pluskat), directed by Bernhard Wicki, were able to intensify the atmosphere of chaos that pervaded the German 7th Army Command on June 6, 1944.

It was Field Marshal Erwin Rommel's comment (spoken by actor Werner Hinz) that gave the film its name. Speaking above the sands of Normandy in early spring 1944, the Field Marshal enunciated his strategy on defeating the invasion:

"Look out there gentleman," he told his subordinates, "how calm, how peaceful it is. A narrow strip of water between the continent and England, between us and the Allies. And beyond that peaceful horizon? A maelstrom! A coiled spring of men, tanks and planes waiting to be unleashed against us. Not a single Anglo-American shall reach the shore. Not a single Anglo-American shall set foot on the beaches. Whenever and wherever it comes, I intend to defeat the invasion right there. Right there, gentlemen, at the water's edge. Believe me, gentlemen, the first twenty-four hours of the invasion will be decisive. For the Allies, as well as Germany, it will be the longest day..., the longest day...."

With his cast assembled, his equipment concentrated at the French ordnance depot in Caen, and his directors on alert for action, Darryl F. Zanuck began phase two.

Andrew "Bundy" Marton, with his singers and 150 Rangers of the U.S. 8th Division, was assigned the task of recreating the 1944 assault on Pointe du Hoc. On D-Day 17 years earlier, Lt. James E. Rudder of the 2nd Ranger Battalion led three companies against the 80-foot cliffs, located on the right flank of Omaha Beach.

Before filming began, a cleanup crew similiar to the Art Department unit employed in Corsica, transformed the plant-overgrown cliffs to their circa 1944 rockiness.

After clearing out 600 live land mines, the crew used flame throwers to burn off the shrubbery and reduce the shrub trees to charcoal. Shell craters were reblasted, a bunker was refurbished and draped with camouflage, and the familiar rubber tires were brought in as burning smoke pots.

Johnny Jendrich's defense force arrived soon after, spending most of their free time drinking wine and calvados, and playing chess with the Rangers. On location, Zanuck had his own canvas chair and a French-built Alouette helicopter standing by, ready to transport him to Gerd Oswald's crew filming in nearby St. Mère Église.

Besides Tommy Sands, Paul Anka and Fabian, the Ranger assault for Marton's camera would include Robert Wagner and George Segal. Wagner had read Ryan's book on his own and hadn't waited to be invited to the filming. He had applied for a part. Moreover, after visiting the American cemetery at Omaha

Beach, he had come to believe that the movie was his personal responsibility. Then too, Zanuck had been luck for him in the past.

The attack on Pointe du Hoc closely resembled the storming of a medieval castle. Following a murderous naval bombardment, the Rangers stormed ashore on a narrow gravel beach. Using mortars to launch hundreds of grappling hooks into the barbed wire nine stories up, the three companies of Ranger extras began their historical climb for the cameras.

The oft-repeated phrase that "three grandmothers with brooms" could have swept the cliff clean is made frighteningly apparent as the Rangers stumble and fall from their ropes and ladders while a small German force keeps them pinned down.

Inevitably there were injuries. Anka suffered a deep cut in his hand, Tommy Sands lacerated his knee and received several stitches, and Wagner injured his back in a collision with Fabian. All the actors, though, had been subjected to a full week's intensive training before Zanuck permitted them to make the actual climb.

For 12 days, Marton filmed the Battle of Pointe du Hoc. Final cost, which included the expense of transporting the Ranger unit to and from their base in Wiesbaden, Germany, was a half a million dollars. Total screen time was less than ten minutes.

On August 13, ominous news reached the unit from Berlin. The Russians had erected a wall between the eastern and western halves of the capital. The Berlin crisis had begun. U.S. Army units throughout Europe were placed on a full alert. At Pointe du Hoc, a direct telephone line to the Ranger's headquarters in Wiesbaden was kept open in case the soldiers were needed in the German capital.

It was during the early days of the Berlin Crisis that a controversy first erupted over the use of American troops in a motion picture production. What originated as a low key congressional request for information later escalated into a major governmental policy revision concerning military cooperation with the motion picture industry.

On September 13, 1961, Representative Robert Wilson, a Republican from California, fired a telegram to Arthur Sylvester, Assistant Defense Secretary for Public Affairs. Prompted by a

Top: *The aftermath of the Vierville breakthrough: a triumphant Brig. Gen. Norman Cota (Robert Mitchum)*. Bottom: *His ankle broken, Lt. Col. John Vandervoort (John Wayne) is wheeled into Ste. Mère Église; at left is Steve Forrest, at right (gesturing) is Stuart Whitman.* — The Longest Day *(20th Century-Fox, 1962)*.

questionable massing of U.S. troops for a Jack Paar telecast from the Berlin Wall, which resulted in disciplinary action against the Army officers, Wilson was anxious to know the extent to which cooperation was being offered Zanuck's crew operating in Normandy.

On October 3, Sylvester defended the use of the Ranger company at Pointe du Hoc: "It was our considered opinion that, basically, such a story has historical importance and that the film will give the public a better understanding of a most crucial combat operation. The film would show the U.S. Armed Forces in gallant action and, although it deals with war in its roughest form, it should prove beneficial for recruiting and in creating general interest in the Armed Forces."

Sylvester further stressed that no violation of Army regulations "apparently" was involved, from the facts obtained via the European command. "The Rangers," he concluded, "were not taken from Berlin, but from elsewhere in Germany. As reported previously, the troops were not paid as extras because the deployment was regarded as an opportunity for the Ranger type troops to participate in cliff scaling training. Consequently, any wages in addition to their military pay would not be justified. As a result of all the facts on hand, there is no thought of reprimanding anyone concerned."

For the moment, members of Congress were satisfied. But the repercussions of the first investigation were already beginning to open the whole spectrum of military cooperation to closer scrutiny. An era was coming to an end, and Darryl Zanuck would soon find himself in the middle of a major policy shift.

To the North, in the little Norman town of Ste. Mère Église, Gerd Oswald prepared to film one of history's most dangerous paratroop landings. Designed to disrupt German communications behind the invasion beaches the night before D-Day, the American airborne landings were a costly success. Although both the 82nd and 101st Airborne divisions accomplished their missions, many paratroopers were drowned in a series of flooded swamplands, shot out of the sky by German antiaircraft guns and often blown by powerful winds miles from their drop zones.

In his book, Cornelius Ryan had concentrated on the catastrophic landing in the town of Ste. Mère Église. In planning the movie battle action, Elmo Williams saw the confrontation where a paratroop company is wiped out, as playing from a unique angle.

"This particular battle," he says, "was laid out specifically from the paratrooper's point of view, every setup in the sequence was vertical, either made from the ground looking up or from the paratrooper's point of view looking down. It was one of those battles that was unique and the only thing that made it unique was having an actor like Red Buttons (portraying Pvt. John Steele) hung up on that church steeple, watching the slaughter below him."

When director Oswald began filming several hand to hand combat sequences on the ground to add realism to the battle, Williams ordered him to stop. "There was nothing wrong with what he was doing," Williams explained, "except that it took away from the pattern we were trying to set, a strictly vertical pattern. There were other battles to film on the ground and we wanted to reserve that type of action for those sequences."

Pressure from Williams and Zanuck was not Oswald's only problem. History was repeating itself as the strong Normandy winds played havoc with the unit's helicopter-borne paratroopers.

"The Normandy winds were simply terrible," laments Oswald. "Our groups, which consisted of about twenty-five French stuntmen, some English paratroopers, and a contingent of soldiers from a nearby French Air Force base, could never land in the proper places. They were always being blown away. Week after week, we had to resign ourselves to getting little pieces of film at a time."

As a last resort, Oswald put in a request for a group of construction cranes. During the last two days of shooting, guidelines were strung and the paratroopers were mechanically dropped on their targets. To further create the illusion of a large scale airborne operation, dummy paratroopers were also dumped from the helicopters. Filming in the actual village where the fateful raid took place gave the sequence its ultimate sense of realism. Throughout the three week filming, the 1500 residents of Ste. Mère Église were given a nightly front row seat at their own history.

Frequently, Zanuck's Alouette would appear, producer and

Normandy winds played havoc with Director Gerd Oswald's shooting schedule; here a parachutist is rescued from the power lines of Ste. Mère Église. — The Longest Day *(20th Century-Fox, 1962).*

director would confer on the progress of the day, and then the special helicopter would wing northeast to Ken Annakin's unit filming near the Orne River Bridge.

By the beginning of September 1961, Marton had completed the Pointe du Hoc sequence and was halfway through the Spitfire strafing attack. Annakin had finished the Orne River assault and was preparing an important train wreck with the

Christian Marquand portrays Commander Philippe Kieffer, leader of the 171 tough French commandos who captured the casino at Ouistreham, a German stronghold. — The Longest Day *(20th Century-Fox, 1962).*

cooperation of the French National Railroad Bureau. Oswald, having finished Ste. Mère Église, was preparing the French commando assault on Ouistreham.

Upon his return from the Corsican landings in June, Elmo Williams had begun the major chore of scouting the locations for the closeup beach landings. These sequences would include both American beach landings, the British landing on Sword, and the French landing at Ouistreham.

With Chomat, an expert French helicopter pilot, at the controls, Williams began to scour Normandy for a town similiar to wartime Ouistreham. "The real Ouistreham," he recalled," lies at the mouth of the Orne River, a very flat uninteresting area, and the casino, the focal point of the French attack, had been ripped down. Since there was nothing left resembling the town the way it was during wartime, Chomat, Oswald and I began to look for a new place where we could get the same effect but in a more confined area that lent itself to dramatization.

"Our first day out we found the perfect location, a town on the coast called Port-en-Bessin. It was perfect because there were still some bombed out buildings in existance. The French mayor, a former member of the resistance (as everybody turned out to be) was delighted to cooperate with us.

"We told him that we wanted to repair the shell holes and then blow them out again. At first, he thought we were crazy, but he eventually gave us all the cooperation he could."

Before filming could begin, though, Oswald went to Zanuck, dissatisfied with William's choice of location. The director, battle-hardened after the disasters in Ste. Mère Église, preferred a small fishing village only three miles from Ouistreham. Faced with a difference of opinion, Zanuck passed the buck to Williams.

"Well, I'm not going to look them over," Zanuck told Williams, "you designed these battle sequences, you can go and check out this other site." Williams and production manager Lee Katz then proceeded to compare the two locations, eventually opting for Port-en-Bessin. Says Oswald, "I was overruled because of a basic logistical problem. My little fishing village was unacceptable because of inadequate housing and catering facilities."

Forced to accept the new location, Oswald penciled in

several changes in Williams' battle plan. The casino, the focal point of German resistance in the town, was constructed at the vertex of two angles, one stretching along an estuary, the other past a ruined castle and some bombed out buildings. The French commando attack could converge on the casino from two sides. Unlike Pointe du Hoc, or Ste. Mère Église, the Ouistreham battle sequence was blocked out horizontally to be one long helicopter shot, here described by Williams: "In the screen version of the attack, you start at the bridge and come down the estuary past the fishing boats. You pull up to the casino, cut right and, near the ruined castle, you see the other attack force. Originally, we planned it differently. You started up beyond the round tower of the castle, and you came down towards the fortified casino. As the attack progressed, the camera panned left, this time revealing the estuary as it came alive with troops."

Quarreling between Williams and Oswald, on the nature of this battle sequence, continued, and when Zanuck finally entered the fracas, Oswald was fired from the picture. Oswald's name does not appear in the final credits; he explains: "In the original contract Darryl had stipulated that each director's contribution had to equal one fourth of the picture to be credited. This was almost impossible to establish, since he was also directing a great deal. But, certainly, the Ste. Mère Église sequence was not a fourth of the film. So, contractually, he could eliminate my name, which he did."

Andrew Marton later completed the Ouistreham sequence under Williams' supervision.

It was during the middle of October that Zanuck was forced to make a fateful decision concerning the proposed filming off the French coast on the Il de Rey.

The tiny islet off the Brittany coast near La Rochelle had been accidentally discovered by Williams during a prolonged search for landing craft. Twenty-four hours later, Zanuck was surveying the bunker strewn beaches, pronouncing the island perfect for closeup beach landings. Before he could mobilize his forces, though, there were two major problems.

One was quite typical for the production: the weather. Winter was coming and it simply was not the time to film a landing sequence off the Brittany Coast. The seasons were changing and massive storms centering in the Central Atlantic could be expected at any time.

Williams preached caution. The logical move was to postpone the exteriors and film them the following spring. But to Zanuck, any postponement spelled disaster. It had taken him six months to gather and organize a vast number of international stars. Could he predict that they would still be available for principle photography eight months from now? Aside from the weather, he had to worry about his financial base, 20th Century-Fox.

Fox was sinking into ruin. The debt for 1961 had been a hefty $22 million. *Cleopatra* was still ridiculously out of control, further draining the monetary reserves of the strife-torn studio. Zanuck began to think rightfully so that should the production be postponed, it might not get started again. He vividly recalled his first confrontation with management.

In the spring of 1961, the Fox executives had launched a powerful assault on *The Longest Day*. One of the prominent board members, John Loeb, demanded that Zanuck take a $3 million loss and get out. But Zanuck would not withdraw, it was stupid for him even to consider it. Author Mel Gussow, in his biography of Zanuck, describes the fateful moment on May 24, 1961 when the producer faced the board:

"Outnumbered, outflanked, and seemingly defeated before he began, Zanuck got up and began fighting with his mouth, which in moments of peril had always been one of his best weapons. He began talking about D-Day, about the world-wide interest in the subject and the limited knowledge that people had about it. This would be the final word on the subject...."

"General James van Fleet (a member of the board) came to Zanuck's rescue. 'He lost his temper,' says Zanuck, 'He practically called them idiots.' He had landed in the first wave on D-Day. Usually at board meetings, he never said anything, but now he said, 'This picture will make more than any other picture.' Then Robert Clarkson began to sway for me. Robert Lehman began to sway for me. They asked me to leave the meeting and wait outside. They then called me in and said I could go ahead, but if I spent more than eight million, they would take my cameras away. I think the vote was six to five in my favor."

With this less than enthusiastic vote of confidence, Zanuck returned to France. That was in the spring. Now, it was the late fall, and the weather factor was launching a more concentrated assault on *The Longest Day*.

In the ballroom of the Hotel Malherb in Caen, in front of his entire crew, Zanuck asked for opinions on whether to postpone or gamble. Predictably, a majority favored postponement. Many of them recalled a similiar situation confronting director Edward Dmytryk's crew on *The Young Lions*, which faced tremendous weather problems in 1956 while filming outside Paris.

Zanuck, fighting for the very life of the studio, was unconvinced. Two days later he told Williams, "I don't trust the weather reports. I think we're through with the worst of it. Get the crews moving and let's finish this picture." John Wayne couldn't have said it any better.

No sooner had Zanuck decided to move his crews to the Il de Rey than another problem surfaced concerning the film's use of American troops. Ever since the Jack Paar incident in Berlin, the Department of Defense had come under increasing scrutiny by Congress in regard to its dealings with the motion picture industry. Although Arthur Sylvester had defended the use of the Ranger company in the filming at Pointe du Hoc, he was still in favor of eliminating the excesses of military cooperation.

Only one week before shooting began on the Il de Rey, Defense Secretary Robert McNamara personally ordered that Zanuck's issue of troops be cut from 700 to 250 men.

A statement from the Pentagon read: "Participation in the film, 'The Longest Day' has been lowered from 700 to 250 at the direction of the Secretary of Defense. This decision was based on the fact that the number originally planned was much larger than is normal in military cooperation. The curtailed participation is being authorized on the basis that it is in the national interest to do so."

The Pentagon decision and a new series of strictly enforced regulations deeply affected the course of future military cooperation with the motion picture industry. It was an historic judgment. For Zanuck, it was another headache.

Luckily, it was the French this time who came to the rescue, ordering over 2000 soldiers to the Il de Rey, to help Zanuck finish his film.

Filming began on October 21, 1961, and stretched for over a month. Zanuck had hauled in his overworked construction crews to rebuild the inhabited portion of Sword Beach on D-Day. Additional machine shops, wardrobe tents and catering facilities were also constructed behind the deserted beaches that looked west toward the stormy Atlantic.

While Marton filmed the American exteriors and Annakin the British, Bernard Wicki, who had been working mostly in Paris on the German interiors, arrived to film the opening shots of Rommel philosophizing above the Normandy bluffs. With the arrival of Jendrich's "Germans" (it was at Omaha Beach that they offered their stiffest resistance), the final phase of action sequences began.

Unlike the Corsican maneuvers, where Zanuck had virtually no direct control over his "extras," at the Il de Rey, the landings were planned on a precise timetable with a group of second assistant directors sprinkled amongst the French assault troops.

Zanuck, himself, describes the first day's shooting on "Omaha Beach": "It was the only time outside the big paratroop jump in Ste. Mère Église, where we had actual casualties. I had about thirty second assistants in uniforms as my squadron leaders. One of the thirty handled each assault group. They picked which 'extras' would fall as casualties, or who would make the beach. We ran a tape from the edge of the shore to the cliff (to form) alleys, so that the men wouldn't bunch up. We then covered the tape with light sand and planted 150 explosives.

"Unfortunately, we never thought about smoke. In the final take, I shot a pistol. That signaled the cameras on the ground and in the air. Bang, it starts and it's the goddamnedest mess I've ever seen in my life.

"They couldn't see because of the smoke. They were bumping into each other ... and we, at the cameras, couldn't see either. People were sitting holding their faces in their hands. Some had facial cuts where they had run into explosives. In one scene, where guys blow up in the air, that wasn't staged. They were running blind. We stayed up all night working out non-smoke or white smoke. I got two takes that were good and decided we wouldn't do it again. We would have killed somebody."

The battle sequences completed, Zanuck withdrew his

crews to Paris. There, in the Boulogne Studios, the producer personally directed many of the final scenes in the film involving the American performers.

Zanuck screened the rough cut of *The Longest Day*, on March 5, 1962. Although he was quite statisfied that the film was the blockbuster needed to revive the sagging fortunes of 20th Century-Fox, he immediately detected that the ending of the film lacked a certain comment on the true meaning of D-Day among the participants. The producer saw that it was time to slow the pace of the film and add one last scene.

A quick phone call was placed to Rome where Richard Burton was courting Elizabeth Taylor both on and off the screen. "I've got a great scene for you," said Zanuck, "can you come up for a couple of days?" Burton agreed to appear as a wounded Spitfire pilot philosophizing on the meaning of war. He treated the short sequence like a scene out of a Shakespearean play. He flew into Paris on April 8th. By that time, the major producton crews had completed their work on the film and had departed. Zanuck personally opened the studio for Burton and a small crew.

The short scene summed up the excitement, exhaustion, courage, confusion, stupidity and horror of D-Day. One of the film's few symbolic moments, it retains a distinct sense of individuality. Burton, his thigh held together with safety pins, lies by the side of a road. Richard Beymer (as Private Dutch Schultz), a lost paratrooper, is exhausted by his night's ordeal. Through all the confusion in trying to wade through a pitched battle and find his unit, he has yet to fire his weapon. Nearby, a dead German officer lies sprawled against a fencepost. ("He was coming to make sure of me," says Burton).

"It's funny," utters Burton, an injection of morphine causing him to slur his words, "He's dead, I'm crippled and you're lost. I suppose it's always like that. I mean war."

An explosion sounds far away. Both hardly stir.

"I wonder who won?" says Beymer. Zanuck smiled as he listed to Beymer's last line. After all, there had never been any doubt in his mind.

4

Freedom Before the Darkness

It is the afternooon of September 21, 1962. For the first time in many weeks, the Alpine foothills are awash in sunshine. High in these meadowlands, not far from the tiny German village of Fussen, a crowd of spectators has gathered.

Along a dirt road that winds through a lush Bavarian pasture, a German catering truck is making labored progress. Visible beyond a little hillock, its steel radial outlined against the Austrian Alps, is a Chapman camera crane. The crane's radial arm carries the words, *The Great Escape.*

The caterer pulls into a makeshift parking lot adjacent to an endless barbed wire fence. He cuts his engine and stares around. Nearby are motorcycles with sidecars, ten-ton Mercedes covered trucks, a Mercedes touring car circa 1940, and fully uniformed German soldiers armed with machine guns and Mauser rifles. Shaking his head in astonishment, the little man turns and presses an electronic horn. The blaring klaxon echoes across the meadow signaling that lunch has arrived. Near the fence and gathered about the Chapman crane is a crowd of nearly a hundred people. A few turn at the sound, but for the most part their attention is riveted on two young men dressed in identical blue sweat-shirts and dirty beige slacks. Actor Steve McQueen and his friend Bud Ekins, a stuntman and motorcycle expert, are standing next to a customized British Triumph racing bike. Comouflaged in Wehrmacht green and disguised as a German BMW, the machine will shortly catapult Ekins over a six foot barbed wire entanglement, a crucial sequence in the 1963 adventure classic, *The Great Escape.*

There is little question that the stunt will succeed. Tim Gibbs, the Australian, has already performed the stunt successfully. Here in the early afternoon sun, Ekins will duplicate the feat for the cameras. Steve McQueen, a well known motorcycle fanatic, must sit this one out. He is simply too valuable, and insurance regulations forbid him to do many of the film's more dangerous motor stunts. Bud Ekins is to be the sacrificial lamb. The pair shake hands and Ekins climbs aboard the converted Triumph. As he revs up the crackling engine, easing up on the throttle, the crowd presses forward. There is electricity in the air, that peculiar magic that surrounds the shooting of a motion picture.

Before he takes off for his final run, Ekins nods to the man atop the Chapman crane. Director John Elliott Sturges turns to his cameraman, Daniel Fapp.

"Okay, this is it," he says blandly. Mentally recording the time on his watch (it is just two o'clock) he adjusts his sun glasses and concentrates intently on the Triumph.

The most difficult challenge of his directing career is almost over. Most of the actors have shot their final scenes and have flown back to their respective countries, and the extras, students from the University of Munich, have returned to their classrooms. It is just a matter of weeks before he, too, can depart for Hollywood to edit and score his masterwork.

In March 1943, the future author of *The Great Escape*, Canadian Paul Brickhill, was flying his Spitfire over the Tunisian Desert in North Africa when his fighter was struck by 20mm cannon fire from an ME-109. His controls shattered and his engine on fire, Brickhill bailed out and was almost immediately captured by the remnants of Rommel's once proud Afrika Korps.

When the Germans evacuated the continent in late March, Brickhill, along with a large group of British and American flyers was transferred to the Italian mainland and from there by train to Sagan, Germany, a small town ninety miles southeast of Berlin in the territory of Silesia, Germany's dustbowl. Carved right out of a nearby forest and erected by Russian prisoners was their final destination: Stalag Luft III.

Brickhill entered the German prisoner of war compound just as its 700 British and American officers were moving into the newly constructed north compound.

Three hundred yards square and surrounded by the latest security precautions, including two nine-foot barbed wire fences, machine gun towers and a fully armed German garrison, the camp was considered escape proof. Squadron leader Roger Bushell's X Organization, an ultra refined escape machine, would soon put the Germans to that test.

Thirty year old Bushell had spent the last three years behind German wire. His captivity had begun on May 23, 1940, when his 12 Spitfires on patrol over the Dunkirk beaches were jumped by 40 twin-engined ME-110s. Bushell claimed two enemy fighters before he was in turn shot down and captured. Three years and several escape attempts later, he was incarcerated in a Gestapo prison until the Luftwaffe had him transferred to Stalag Luft III. He was never the same again, as Brickhill observes in an early chapter of *The Great Escape:*

"This was a changed Roger, not the old boisterous soul who thought escape was good, risky sport like skiing.... Now he was moodier, and the gaze from that twisted eye was more foreboding. In Berlin, he'd seen the Gestapo torturing people and he could not tolerate Germans anymore.... His frustrated energy was beginning to focus on the people responsible for his captivity. He cursed all Germans indiscriminately ... but inside was a clear, cool-headed hatred and it found sublimation in outwitting them...."

As Big X, it would be Bushell who would plan and execute "The Great Escape."

Paul Brickhill became one of 700 Allied prisoners of war who worked for Bushell's escape machine. As a cog in the machine, he bossed a gang of stooges who guarded the camp forgers working in their exposed position at the hut windows. Brickhill was all set to escape with 250 others when Bushell excluded him because of claustrophobia.

On the moonless night of March 23, 1944, the squadron leader executed his plan. Supplied with forged identity papers and civilian clothes, 76 officers broke out of Stalag Luft III through an elaborate tunnel and made a brief but spectacular dash across Germany for freedom.

Two weeks later Bushell and 49 others were recaptured and murdered by the Gestapo. Only three officers escaped to England; the rest were returned to Stalag Luft III and other prisons, including the Sachsenhausen Concentration Camp.

The tragedy redoubled the prisoners' desire for freedom. Brickhill helped engineer a new tunnel, which by July 1944 was creeping out under the campground towards the wire. But in January 1945, before it was completed, the Germans evacuated the camp to avoid the advancing Russian winter offensive. The prisoners were forcemarched 60 miles to Spemberg and then taken by cattle truck to the German seaport of Bremen where they were settled in an old condemned camp.

The Germans were soon under attack from two sides, however, and the prisoners were moved once again. Brickhill describes their final days of captivity: "We were sheltered in barns up near Lubeck when we heard the barrage as the British First Army crossed the Elbe River. Two days later on May 2nd, we heard firing down the road and two tanks rumbled through the trees from the south. We didn't know whether they were Germans or British and you could practically see the nerves sticking out of everyone's skin and vibrating like piano wire. The hatch of the first tank opened and two Tommies stuck their heads out. We ran up to them screaming at the top of our voices."

After his discharge, Brickhill resumed writing, concentrating on stories about the Royal Air Force and prisoner escapes. It took him four and half years to finish *The Great Escape*.

Twice after the war, he returned to Germany to research the actual sites of the tragedy, and once he was given permission by the Soviet Union to cross the Iron Curtain and walk through the scenes of the murders. After the principal Gestapo chiefs were hanged in 1948, Brickhill leafed through several thousand pages of unpublished reports, including those of Wing Commander Bowes of the RAF Special Investigation Branch, who conducted the postwar investigation into the crimes. The last quarter of the novel was devoted to the aftermath of the escape. He then searched out the important survivors and filled in the few gaps left.

First published by W.W. Norton & Company in August 1950, *The Great Escape* became a rousing testament to the freedom and spirit of mankind. The intricacies of the drama were later incorporated into many British screenplays about the war including the popular 1957 drama, *The Colditz Story*.

Despite the surefire dramatic qualities of his story, Brickhill adamantly refused to sell the novel to filmmakers. He spurned lucrative offers and promises to treat the material factually, claiming that it was simply not his story to sell and that there were too many others involved, including the families of the slain officers who preferred to forget the horrible wartime tragedy.

He was quite satisfied with his book royalties and felt he had been justly compensated for his research. There was no reason to carry the project further.

He continued to write about prisoner of war escapism (*Escape or Die* in 1952) and when the punitive British taxation system proved unbearable, he moved to Australia. *The Great Escape* went through four printings in eight years and in March 1961 the Fawcett World Library purchased the paperback rights. As late as 1960, Brickhill was still declining motion picture offers. Meanwhile 8000 miles away, a hard driving Hollywood director was trying to kindle interest in the very book that Brickhill wished forgotten.

Army Air Corps 1st Lt. John Sturges was in Washington when the March 1944 breakout from Stalag Luft III occurred. Barely three months before D-Day, he was sweating out his transfer overseas to an Air Corps Photographic Unit. On direct orders from General Henry "Hap" Arnold, Sturges was to accompany director William Wyler to Corsica where the pair would create *Thunderbolt*, a brilliant documentary detailing the life of a typical P-47 fighter bomber sqaudron operating against German troop and supply concentrations in Northern Italy.

A film editor at RKO studios before the war, Sturges was on detached service from the 1st Motion Picture Base Unit in Culver City, California. Like many Hollywood film technicians, he had spent the early years of the war editing scores of military training films, both at "Fort Roach" in Culver City, and at Wright Field, Ohio.

On June 9, 1944, he arrived in Caserta, 20 miles north of Naples. Rome had been liberated and the Allies were moving inland from the Normandy beaches. To prevent the resupply of German units still deployed to the north of Rome, Air Force General Ira Eaker, commander in chief of Allied Air Forces, Mediterranean, was planning Operation Strangle, an aerial offensive that would become the primary focus of *Thunderbolt*.

In Caserta, Wyler asked for and received permission to

The chief: Director and Producer John Sturges, who spent over ten years attempting to launch production of The Great Escape *(UA, 1963).*

work with a front line fighter bomber squadron. Two weeks later Sturges was on Corsica attached to the 12th Combat Camera Unit. For the next nine months they filmed numerous raids from the windows of a converted B-25 Mitchell bomber that bristled with cameras. Following the chubby P-47s over the Mediterranean and on to their targets over the port of Spezia won Wyler's unit four battle stars and a Unit Citation.

After his discharge from the Air Corps in early 1946,

Sturges worked as an assistant director at Columbia Pictures, and it was there under Harry Cohn's tutelage that he directed his first film, *The Man Who Dared*. He later transferred to Metro Goldwyn Mayer, where he was signed on as a contract director. In the summer of 1950 he picked up a copy of *Reader's Digest* and began reading the serialization of *The Great Escape*. To this day, his original fascination with the story remains unchanged.

Says Sturges, "It was the perfect embodiment of why our side won! Here was the German military machine, the sparkling uniforms and the absolute obedience to orders. On the other side of the wire, there were men from every country, every background, makeup and language, doing everything they pleased. With no arbitrary rules, they voluntarily formulated an organization which eventually clobbered the German machine."

While reading through the Brickhill novel for the first time, Sturges recalled an incident in Italy that reinforced his belief in the novel's valid theme. During a tourist visit to the front lines, he was delayed in a massive tieup at a rural intersection where an American PFC was directing traffic. A general arrived by jeep and demanded the right of way. According to Sturges, the PFC shouted, "Sorry bud, you'll have to wait your turn!"

"By the side of the road," he recalled, "I noticed this small group of German prisoners. One of them was a captain, which was a high rank in the Wehrmacht. He saw what was going on and I knew he understood English because he was reading an American Superman comic book. What I saw in the German's face was utter disbelief, the whole collapse of what he'd been led to believe."

Convinced that *The Great Escape* was the perfect film project, Sturges decided to go right to the top. On a pleasant sunny Southern California day, he drove to the MGM lot with the express purpose of selling the novel to Louis B. Mayer. He was embarking on a crusade that would stretch through 13 years of his life.

Contract directors are not part of the upper strata of studio hierarchy, and it had taken Sturges a long time to get an appointment with Mayer. And when the meeting finally occurred, it was brief and disturbing. In a nutshell, Mayer and his studio executives were disquieted by the story's tragic climax.

"What the hell kind of a great escape is this?" they

chorused, "no one escapes! Even if we did change the ending, how could we tell a unified story with so many characters and entangling elements. This will be another ten million dollar film. Forget it!"

Sturges could not forget it. He remained convinced that the project was workable. It would just take time. Through the grapevine, he had already learned that Brickhill was rejecting film offers in his own country and he was confident that only he, John Sturges, could convince the author to let his story be filmed.

After each of his increasingly prestigious films, *Bad Day at Black Rock* in 1954, *Gunfight at the OK Corral* in 1957, *The Old Man and the Sea* in 1958 and *Never So Few* in 1959, Sturges tried to interest producers in his pet project, but met with virtually the same negative response each time.

Impressed with the new freedom of his free lance director friends, Sturges left MGM in 1959 and signed a partnership agreement with the Mirisch Company, one of Hollywood's first successful independent production entities.

It was here among associates William Wyler, Robert Wise and John Ford, that he found the creative freedom he had been seeking. The Mirisch Brothers shrewdly gave complete autonomy over their productions to a group of directors considered to be Hollywood's finest. All financial and distribution responsibility, however, remained with the brothers.

During the period when the major studios were becoming more and more cautious about fostering and financing ambitious and expensive film projects, the Mirisch brothers and their distribution partner, United Artists, continued to offer freedom to their creative people. *West Side Story, One, Two, Three,* and *The Children's Hour* were a few of their successful films of the period.

Sturges' first project was *The Magnificent Seven*, a film that won worldwide success and became a western classic. With a group of virtually unknown actors (Steve McQueen, James Coburn, Charles Bronson, and Horst Bucholz) Sturges established a clarity of character and sense of pace rarely achieved in the western genre. The film won for Sturges the mandate to produce *The Great Escape*.

In the spring of 1960, he met with the Mirisch Brothers and Arthur Krim and Robert Benjamn of United Artists. An agreement was reached to advance Sturges the desired front money to purchase *The Great Escape* and hire a screenwriter to adapt it. It was generally agreed that another multi-character adventure like *The Magnificent Seven* was commercially attractive, especially if Sturges could successfully integrate many of his young actors into the new project.

Immediately, Surges wrote a letter to Brickhill in Australia, describing his decade long campaign to sell the project. The Britisher, who previously had considered the thought of selling his novel to the money-mad Yanks an outrageous move, agreed to meet Sturges in Hollywood and discuss the project.

Sturges treated Brickhill with mink gloves. He promised there would be no half measures in the telling of the story. Everything would be filmed just as it happened and Brickhill, responding to the director's honesty and sincerity, agreed to sell his novel to Sturges and to become a partner in the venture.

With Brickhill's help, Sturges located Wally Floody, the former "Tunnel King" of Stalag Luft III, who was signed on as the film's technical advisor. He also obtained the cooperation and help of senior British officers Wings Day and Group Captain Massey. In South Africa, he convinced the parents of Roger Bushell that their son's death would be treated with proper taste and given a sense of history.

Sturges gave the task of preparing the screen treatment to William Roberts who had previously worked on *The Magnificent Seven* with writer Walter Newman.

In *The Great Escape*, Brickhill had concentrated on facts and events rather than characterization. The Allied officers in Stalag Luft III were necessarily overshadowed by the bizarre elements of the escape. To create a scenario that would breed effective audience identification and give substance to the breakout, Robert's task was to flesh out Brickhill's one-dimensional freedom seekers.

Knowing that for security precautions only 12 men had actually known the entire escape plan, Sturges asked his writer to reduce the principal participants to about a dozen officers and to tell the story entirely through their eyes. He also gave Roberts a scrapbook in which the Brickhill book was cut apart, pasted onto individual pages and divided into sections, each one describing a

separate entity, such as tunnels, traps, the camp itself, Big X, the scroungers, the tailors, the manufacturers, the forgers, the stooges, the Gestapo, the ferrets, etc. The scrapbook became an indispensable tool.

The problems confronting Roberts were quite similar to those he had faced on *The Magnificent Seven*. Says Roberts, "In *The Great Escape* we needed an authority figure like the Yul Brynner character in *The Magnificent Seven*. By telling a great deal of the action through his eyes, we could in turn introduce other characters. Luckily, we had the cool calculating Big X as a handy mold."

In his 64 page treatment, Big X dominates. Roberts also developed characters that became the future prototypes for "the cooler king," the American scrounger, the Royal Navy dispersal chief and the limping senior British officer.

In the meantime, Sturges had begun filming *By Love Possessed*, with Lana Turner and Efrem Zimbalist, Jr. He again ran into script difficulties, and once more Roberts came to his rescue, helping unravel and coordinate the enormously complex James Gould Cozzens novel. Since Roberts had completed his primary task, *The Great Escape* treatment, Sturges began searching for another writer to carry the ball further and develop a shooting script.

In an elevator at Columbia Pictures, Sturges bumped into Walter Newman. After a moment of uncomfortable silence (their stormy relationship on *The Magnificent Seven* was still fresh in their memory), Sturges discussed his new project. "It's about a group of American and British flyers escaping from a German Stalag. I'd like you to take a look at the book and consider doing a script."

It sounded good to Newman and he accepted the assignment. While he too was concerned with the one-dimensional characters, the majority of his time was spent in workably dramatizing the complicated events of the escape. Once the technical flow of the film was completed, he hoped to backtrack and flesh out the characters. But although his character names do

---

Facing page: *The two top American stars Steve McQueen (left) and James Garner discuss a scene with Director John Sturges.* — The Great Escape *(UA, 1963)*

appear in the final film, Newman was not to complete his script.

He later complained, "It was extremely difficult to work with John. He was working on so many projects. And even when we did work together, he failed to concentrate his ideas and present them in usable form."

A schism occurred when the normally complacent Mirisch Brothers demanded to see a portion of Newman's unfinished script. Sturges found himself torn between divided loyalties. In order to secure the proper commitments from actors like James Garner and Steve McQueen, he needed to negotiate now and the Mirisch's could not deal without a script. On the other hand, the last thing he wanted to do was antagonize Newman whom he considered a fine writer and who needed time to finish his first draft.

The script was at last progressing and with two new films coming up for him in the near future, Sturges was too busy to interrupt his writer's productivity. It was an exasperated Newman who solved the director's problem by departing for another assignment.

Although the first draft satisfied the Mirisch Brothers, who immediately signed McQueen and Garner, it was hardly the polished shooting script Sturges needed. It was overly long and lacked central continuity. Several times, Newman had followed the novel into sidetracking subplots. Since Newman had been denied the opportunity to backtrack, the characters weren't yet completely developed and well rounded.

A constructionist was needed, someone who could tighten the Newman script and eliminate some of the unnecessary subplots. W.R. Burnett's name was mentioned, for, in his novel *The Asphalt Jungle*, a famous crime novel of the 1950's, Burnett had dealt quite successfully with a multicharacter story. Actor Frank Sinatra brought the pair together in the spring of 1961 by hiring them both to create *Sergeants Three*, a satirical comedy western remake of Rudyard Kipling's *Gunga Din*, starring Sinatra and his Rat Pack.

During the script stage on the latter film, Sturges phoned Burnett and invited him to his home in Studio City where "The Great Headache" was being reorganized. Having heard about the film, Burnett was eager to apply his skill to the script, so much so in fact that he slammed a car door on his thumb on the way over.

He arrived at the director's home with his thumb in a painful splint but ready to talk business.

Sturges greeted the writer and showed him the two previous aborted scripts. "Bill," he said, "I'm getting nowhere fast on this project. The Mirisch Brothers are being as patient as possible, but since we're most likely going to be shooting next spring, time is running out. There's something of value in both of these scripts but I need your help to pull it together, and make it work. Can you do it?"

Despite the pain in his thumb, Burnett gripped Sturges' offered palm firmly. Writer number three was about to put his talents to the test.

Screenwriter W.R. Burnett ripped Newman's script apart, developing a straight line narrative that emphasized the complexities of the tunnel operation. As *The Great Escape* was destined to benefit from sharp cutting, Burnett began developing short penetrating scenes that pinpointed action and introduced character. He felt that narration (a technique used extensively by both previous writers) was unnecessary if the scenes were simply composed and realistic in nature.

After the completion of *Sergeants Three* in September 1961, Sturges began a closer relationship with his writer, the result being that the pair spent a great deal of time developing the humorous interplay between the film's three American characters, Hendley, Hilts and Goff, and their British compatriots.

Once Burnett's first draft was completed, Sturges sent off copies to his first two choices for the crucial role of Big X — John Mills and Richard Harris. Mills, a veteran British actor who had appeared in *The Colditz Story* declined the offer, claiming in part that the material lacked a certain freshness. Harris, a much younger actor, whom Sturges had found excellent in his role opposite Marlon Brando in *Mutiny on the Bounty* fell in love with the role of Big X and accepted the assignment, provided he could finish *This Sporting Life* for director Karel Reisz.

It was after his interview with Harris that Sturges considered hiring yet another writer to work on the script. Something in Burnett's final draft bothered him and it wasn't the writer's fault. Richard Harris had pointed out that it was obvious that somewhere between Brickhill and Burnett, the English feeling of the story had been lost. Sturges was now worried that such an error could ultimately affect the authenticity of the film. Assistants Robert Relyea and Jack Reddish, both competent second unit directors, were already preparing to scout locations for the second unit in Germany. Time was of the essence.

So, in February 1962, Sturges hired James Clavell, a former resident of Japan's Changi Prison during World War II and the future author of *King Rat* and *Shogun*, to redevelop the English characters in *The Great Escape*, particularly Big X, and instill in their makeup a properly English philosophy and bearing.

Clavell brought forth Big X's most important characteristics, namely his ruthless hatred of the enemy and an overwhelming desire to "mess up the works." It was during Clavell's tenure on the script that Sturges decided once more to change the film's principle focus and reduce the importance of Big X to just another one of the 12 leading characters, giving him equal billing with the two Americans.

For his next film project, *A Girl Named Tamiko*, Sturges, producer Hal Wallis, cameraman Charles Lang and a unit of hand-picked specialists traveled to Japan in the winter of 1961 and spent weeks selecting and photographing every location called for in the script. This photography was later matched entirely on the Samuel Goldwyn Studios backlot.

Sturges planned to follow the same pattern for *The Great Escape*. He revealed to reporters on February 19, 1962, that only 10 percent of the film was to be shot abroad. The camp itself was to be constructed in the San Gabriel Mountains near Big Bear Lake, a two hour drive from Hollywood.

With such a plan in mind, Sturges assembled his scouting unit which consisted of old friends Robert Relyea and Jack Reddish (Relyea had worked on both *Never So Few* and *The Magnificent Seven*), and art director Fernando Carrera. The trio arrived in Munich in the middle of February and working out of a rented office at the Geisel Gasteig Studios, they circled Germany twice in search of potential locations.

Relyea applied to the American consul for permission to visit Sagan, but the Cold War had escalated and the authorities were reluctant to allow any Americans into the Russian Sector. The scouting unit would have to rely solely on photographs and the help of their technical advisers.

After the first scouting trip, the group received ominous news from Sturges in Hollywood. The Pandora's Box opened by entertainer Jack Parr the previous summer when American troops were exploited during a television broadcast in Berlin, and the situation with Darryl F. Zanuck's *The Longest Day*, which was demanding regiments of extras for use in huge battle scenes, were causing problems for producers with potential need for military extras.

The military would not cooperate with Sturges in Hollywood so plans were now being formulated to use a large group of college students and nonprofessionals to avoid the cost of hiring professional extras. "Impossible!" came the response from the Screen Extras Guild. There was a standing rule, they pointed out, that all productions filmed within a 300 mile radius of the corner of Hollywood and Vine, must hire professional extras exclusively. There were to be no exceptions. Faced with such a prohibitive cost, Sturges reluctantly decided to take the entire film abroad.

In April 1962, he arrived in Germany with another crew. The basic problem now was where to build the camp. Since Geisel Gasteig Studios was located out in the Bavarian countryside, amid forested frontier, Sturges soon found that he could construct the camp virtually on the backlot. There was snow on the ground when he first spied his location. He brought the studio president out to see his choice and was quickly told that there were tiny pine saplings beneath the snow. "It seems that the American director had stumbled upon a thriving parcel of the German National Forest," said the amused executive.

Since the location was so ideal, being only a few hundred yards from the sound stages where Carrera was already designing the huge tunnel sets, Sturges decided to send Relyea to the German minister of the interior for permission to remove the trees.

Relyea found the minister in Munich and brought him out to the studio where Sturges took him aboard a Chapman crane, showing him the area planned for the prison camp exterior. The minister was told that the studio would replant the trees elsewhere, two for one, and as the saplings were still young and could be safely removed, the minister agreed to the deal. After Sturges' crew finished in Germany, the prison camp was dismantled and the vacant area was replanted. Today, it is a thriving forest.

In early May, Richard Harris withdrew from the project. Having read the new Clavell script, he became dissatisfied with his deflated role as Big X. In any case, *This Sporting Life* (in which Harris portrayed a British soccer player) was badly behind schedule and Harris couldn't possibly meet Sturges' deadlines.

To replace Harris, Sturges signed veteran British actor Richard Attenborough, who was exuberant over the part. Despite its new perspective as simply one of the many officers in the escape plot, Attenborough was still fascinated by Big X, a flying officer, who despite torture, constant threats, and the crucial responsibility of command, continued to defy his captors in every way possible, retaining his fiery passion to the very end.

With principle photography scheduled for the first week in June 1962, Sturges had already gathered the remainder of his crew in Munich. Daniel Fapp, a Mirisch Company cinematographer who had just returned from Geisel Gasteig where Billy Wilder had completed *One, Two, Three,* was assigned to Sturges on Robert Relyea's advice (the pair had worked together on *West Side Story*).

Sturges chose his stuntmen carefully. At Steve McQueen's suggestion, it had been decided that the Hilts character would steal a German motorcycle during the escape. The director liked the idea, because of its historical validity, and although a motorcycle had not been used in the March 1944 escape, there was proof that escaping prisoners had in some cases stolen motorcycles.

The prisoners had gotten the idea from the French Underground, as Sturges relates: "What they would do was wait until nightfall along the forest roads where the dispatch cars ran. No one knew who rode in them, high brass or couriers, but they would often travel like a bat out of hell with motorcycle guards front and rear. The French quickly got the notion of stretching piano wire across the road at a 45 degree angle terminating in a gulley. They would let all these fellows pass by and then lift the wire on the last rider who was immediately clobbered.

"By the time the next to last guy looked around, they would

Facing page: *Squadron leader Roger Bartlett (Richard Attenborough) instructs his X organization (visible faces, from left: Pleasance, McCallum, Layton, Garner, Bronson, Nigel Stock, Unknown, Coburn, Unknown, Attenborough, James Donald, Jackson).* — The Great Escape *(UA, 1963).*

be gone. Since the couriers ran on strict timetables, it was dangerous for him to turn around and search for his buddy. He usually just kept right on going."

Since McQueen was already a highly capable motorcycle rider, Sturges gave him authority to purchase the motorcycles and hire a stuntman. The actor immediately contacted his good friend Bud Ekins who operated a North Hollywood motorcycle repair shop. Ekins was hired as chief motorcycle stuntman.

Before he left for four months in Germany, Ekins purchased two British Triumph motorcycles and began the major camouflage job that would turn them into German bikes. Here he describes the conversion, which took only ten hours of work: "I gave them both a solo seat, a rack in the back and a different front fender that was flared like the German bikes. I put special competition forks in them and I rigged the suspension like racing bikes of the period. Finally, I painted them both Army green and gave them a balsa wood battery." The motorcycles completed, Ekins and three others, Chuck Hayward, Roy Sichner and Roy Jensen, left for Munich, arriving at Geisel Gasteig Studios on June 8, 1962.

Despite the rainstorms that pelted Germany throughout the spring and summer of 1962, creating seas of mud in the newly cleared backlot, Fernando Carrera completed the camp on time. The barracks themselves were merely shells with no interior, but there was no denying the camp's overall realism.

Said actor Jud Taylor who portrayed Goff the American, "It was really impressive, because when you came out of the woods into this clearing there really was a camp with towers and barbed wire. I was walking out there one afternoon and I saw this man walking his dog through the woods. He looked very distressed when he saw the camp. He didn't know where it had come from and it wasn't until I told him in broken German that it was a movie set that he was relieved."

Beyond the trees and only a thousand feet from the camp were the sound stages where Carrera had constructed the tunnel sets. Brickhill had been very explicit in describing the underground escape route. Organized and designed after years of trial and error, the tunnels dug by the X Organization were the most modern ever seen and served to give X the final film its authenticity and sense of claustrophobia.

Top: *Hilts (Steve McQueen) finds himself in the Cooler once again.* Bottom:
"Tunnel Kings" Willy (John Layton, left) and Danny (Charles Bronson). — The
Great Escape *(UA, 1963).*

Extending along the entire length of a stage, the tunnels were constructed with wood and skins filled with plaster and dirt, simulating the dirt interiors. To photograph the prisoners as they scurried through the tunnels on their underground trolley system, a dolly track was constructed. For other camera angles, Carrera built U-shaped tunnels. On another soundstage, he constructed the full sized barracks rooms where the prisoners toiled and slept.

In nearby Munich, the theatrical center of Germany, Sturges found his German actors. The handsome Hannes Messemer was signed to play the critical role of the camp commandant, Colonel Von Luger. During World War II, Messemer was captured by the Russians on the Eastern Front, and escaped by walking hundreds of miles to the German border, a feat duplicated by few Germans.

For the role of Werner, the chronically nervous ferret, Sturges found Robert Grief, who despite the loss of an arm to cancer, was superb as the innocent young German later blackmailed by Hendley (James Garner). For Straachwitz, the menacing sergeant who brandishes a Schmeisser submachine gun as readily as a clipboard, the director signed musical comedy star Harry Riebauer.

Til Kiwe, who portrayed Frick the Ferret, who discovers one of the escape tunnels, was another former P.O.W. who spent most of the war as prisoner of the Americans in Arizona, an interesting existence described by Relyea who knew Kiwe well: "Kiwe came from our own Stalag Luft III in the Arizona desert. This was where we kept our own rotten eggs and interestingly enough, he made seventeen escape attempts from that camp. He used to tell us how he and his mates contemplated escaping to California, stealing aboard a freighter and making it back to the war zone."

Another fine German actor was Robert Freitag, who portrayed Captain Posen, Von Luger's adjutant. It was a small role, but as Relyea points out, John Sturges excelled at casting excellent actors in supporting roles. "John's theory has always been to put superb actors into the so-called gut of the picture. When he

---

Facing page: *"We can get out when the lights go down," whispers Hendley (James Garner, right) to Mac Donald (Gordon Jackson, left), Colin Blythe (Donald Pleasance), and Big X (Richard Attenborough).* — The Great Escape *(UA, 1963).*

to put superb actors into the so-called gut of the picture. When he has a critical role, he will usually fall back on the finest actor he can find for the part. In one of his early films, *Bad Day at Black Rock*, the heavies were Robert Ryan, Ernest Borgnine, and Lee Marvin, and audiences weren't familiar with the work of two of those actors. Yet, they gave excellent performances that contributed heavily to the success of the film."

A career article later published on Sturges in *Films and Filming* magazine expanded on Sturges' casting talent. "He is not a director with a notable talent for deep or penetrating character studies. But he is marvelously adept at establishing the identity and individuality of his characters, even minor ones, with a few telling, economical touches (aided certainly by his excellent eye for casting actors with strong and distinctive personalities). Here, as in all his best films, we come to be involved with and concerned for the escapees, and in this instance to root for them...."

June 4, 1962, dawned cold, dark and foreboding. At approximately 7:00 a.m. Sturges arrived at Geisel Gasteig in a driving rainstorm. There was snow on the ground, and the work of the flamethrower trucks the previous day had done little but create more mud and slush in the prison compound.

All thoughts of filming exteriors discarded, the director called a meeting of the cast and crew to decide what to do. So as not to waste valuable time, the crew voted to go indoors and begin filming *The Great Escape* somewhere in the middle of the picture. Even if the rain did let up, it was virtually impossible to work in the mud: once the dry season arrived, the cameras could never match the two settings.

Actors James Garner and Donald Pleasance (who was playing Blythe the Forger) were given their call and Sturges began shooting in one of the cavernous Geisel Gasteig sound stages where Carrera had hastily erected the interior of a prison barracks.

It continued to rain for several days and Sturges began to wonder whether he would ever see the sun again. Two weeks later the weather did improve enough to begin shooting exteriors, in this case the film's opening where the prisoners arrive at the camp.

Facing page: *The last moments of Ashley-Pitt (David McCallum).* — The Great Escape *(UA, 1963).*

Relyea and Reddish had already gathered the motorized equipment necessary for the opening. There were motorcycles with side cars, big Mercedes truck transports, two Mercedes touring cars (convertibles) and also two Volkswagen command jeeps, altogether some 60 vehicles. The arrival sequence was eventually finished on the network of roads to the west of Geisel Gasteig.

Interestingly, in the Burnett script, which followed the Brickhill novel closely, the film had opened differently, showing the way in which many of the flyers were actually captured. In addition, the promotion department of United Artists had asked that Burnett work some women into the story.

"We had several openings," says Burnett. "In one, Hendley, our American scrounger, was shacking up with a German girl who had said 'the hell with Germany,' when the Gestapo broke into their house and sent him off to prison. We also had a scene showing Big X being worked over by the Gestapo. In the original script, we also went into greater detail with the Ashley-Pitt character (portrayed by a pre-"Man from U.N.C.L.E." David McCallum). He was portrayed very snobbishly as the upper class Britisher, third son of a Duke. Eventually, though, he became a hero by killing the Gestapo chief and saving Big X and Mac Donald (Gordon Jackson) from capture. The hero came through in the film, but the snobbery was eventually lost when the script proved too long."

A month after shooting began, Relyea was still getting letters from United Artists asking politely that they put more women in the story. "One," he recalled, "said that we might be guaranteed big box office if when David McCallum was killed in the train station, he could be cradled in the lap of a beautiful girl wearing a low cut blouse and showing a lot of leg. They even wanted us to select her by organizing a Miss Prison Camp contest in Munich." Whatever the commercial possibilities, Sturges would have nothing of this publicity department hokum.

In July, Steve McQueen suddenly decided that his part was too small and weak and confusing. In Clavell's shooting script Hilts is introduced in the film's opening sequence when he discovers a blind spot in the wire, carries on in the "mole manuever," an aborted escape attempt with Flying Officer Ives (Angus Lennie), spends a great deal of time in the cooler, and then disappears after Ive's death on the wire. He reappears in the escape tunnel, but there is nothing of Steve McQueen for nearly 30 minutes of film.

Conscious of this, he confronted Sturges with a plea for at least a couple of scenes to keep his character going in the "gut" of the film. Sturges admitted that there had been an oversight, but asked McQueen to continue until they could work out some additional scenes. "Nothing doing," was the actor's reply. Seasoned after his confrontation with Paramount Pictures the previous summer on *Hell Is for Heroes*, McQueen knew that he could demand certain reasonable benefits; the greater development of his character seemed a modest request.

But Sturges hedged. To add scenes at this point was impossible. The script was ridiculously overlong and with the weather so erratic, production was already behind schedule. He considered eliminating the Hilts character altogether, having his actions absorbed by other characters.

As the rift grew, there were rumors that McQueen had been fired. Then each side regrouped. By telegram, the Mirisch Brothers informed Sturges that United Artists considered McQueen indispensable and that if any additional money was needed to hire a new writer, it would be forthcoming. Meanwhile, James Garner and Bud Ekins had cornered McQueen asking him to simmer down and be patient with Sturges. Both placations had the desired effect. McQueen cooled off and returned to work while Sturges, with United Artists' backing, hired Ivan Moffit in London to do some rewriting.

Moffit, a veteran screenwriter, was between jobs, having just completed *Tender Is the Night* for 20th Century-Fox. He arrived in Munich soon after and for ten days, while the crew continued to shoot exteriors, the script was reworked and expanded.

Moffit created the scene in which Big X asks Hilts to break out through his "blind spot," chart the land beyond the trees, record the information and then smuggle it back into the camp by deliberately turning himself in. By creating such an interplay Moffit forced a natural collision between Big X's "escape at all costs" attitude and Hilts' hardbitten individualism. The confrontation which included Hilts' line, "I wouldn't do that for my own mother!" is quite comical in the final script.

Satisfied with his character's new found identity, McQueen worked hard, contributing a great deal to the final film. In a role similiar to that of Buzz Rickson in *The War Lover*, McQueen excells as the "hot shot" American pilot who insults the Germans, has no patience for the British, and who devotes all of his thoughts towards escape. The motorcycle chase where Hilts leads half the German Army on a wild chase was the perfect coup de grace and gave the film an overflowing sense of movement.

After two months in the camp, Sturges prepared his crew for location shooting. Since he was already running out of money, the escape sequences could not be as elaborate as originally planned. Instead of filming through many cities and villages, simulating the prisoners' race for freedom, Sturges decided to concentrate his location sequences in and around the small town of Füssen, about 180 miles southeast of Munich near the Austrian border.

In the little town, which the scouting unit had previously found desirable, he found everything he needed, a train station, narrow streets, a distinct Alpine quality (in the film the prisoners are making for Switzerland), a little river, and, not far away, meadowlands—in short, "motorcycle country."

Bud Ekins was by now eager to work on the motorcycle stunts. His first assignment was to trip the German rider so Hilts can steal his motorcycle, but Sturges' hope that a motorcycle rider could be tripped right into a gulley seemed impossible. "Something," says Ekins, "must have been lost in the translation because when a rider hits the wire, he's going to fall off the bike and that's it. But John wanted the feeling of the bike coming at the wire, changing directions and then flying off into a ditch. He just wasn't satisfied with the bike plopping down in the middle of the highway."

In order to take advantage of some intricate shadows, Sturges had hoped to find a patch of road enclosed by trees. Since such a setting was unavailable, the scenes was shot on a stretch of open highway outside Füssen.

Throttling up to 40 miles an hour, Ekins would fly off the bike trying to land in a ditch, but each time he would only end up on the road with a sore behind. Tom Gibbs, an Australian "scrambler," was given the chance at the stunt. On his first try Gibbs

Assistant Director Robert Relyea relaxes in the Bavarian meadowlands during shooting of the motorcycle chase. — The Great Escape *(UA, 1963).*

skidded the bike fifty feet down the highway and Relyea, who was handling the logistics of this sequence under Sturges' supervision, thought it was perfect.

Relyea turned to the director, "John we can arrange this with a simple cut. We'll just switch from the skid to a shot showing the bike hitting the ditch."

Gibbs limped over and asked if his stunt was good enough. "It's fine," said Relyea, "but could you try it once more?"

Ekins hurried over and slapped the Australian on the back, "Come on, they're paying you good money for this!" Gibbs grunted and did the stunt twice more for the cameras. For the role of the unlucky German rider, he also dumped the bike into a roadside ditch.

Leaving Relyea to coordinate the next motorcycle sequence, which included a chase through a little village on the outskirts of Füssen (simulating a German Army checkpoint), Sturges returned to the Geisel Gasteig Studios to arrange cooperation with the German National Railroad Bureau for the train sequences.

Outside Munich, he was assigned a "special" and Carrera's art department went to work. On one of the passenger cars they fitted platforms designed to accommodate the huge arc lamps that would illuminate the train interiors where the escaping prisoners would be nervously seated. On one flat car, Sturges mounted his

Chapman crane, which was designed to swing out over the passenger car and film the jump by two stuntmen doubling for Garner and Pleasance who are forced to leave the train when the Gestapo arrive. Carrera outfitted the remaining flatcar with the wardrobe and hairdressing equipment.

When his train was rolling, the railroad bureau attached a special radio operator to the camera crew who would alert the engineer as to any potential traffic on the main line. "We had to squeeze our shooting schedule between actual runs," says Sturges. "So they would organize our times and we'd go out on a section of track, run a certain distance and then retreat to a siding just as another passenger train raced by at eighty miles an hour."

When the multifaceted railroad sequences were finished, John Sturges went looking for a Luftwaffe aerodrome for yet another escape vignette. In early September, he found one north of Munich. Although it was equipped with the latest jet aircraft, the field also boasted a complement of AT-6 training planes, the all purpose aircraft that film makers constantly substituted for available enemy fighters, in this case those carrying German insignia. In Florida that same month, Warner Brothers was using similiar AT-6s for Japanese zero fighters launching winged assaults on a naval base for their feature film, *PT 109*.

In the aerodrome scene, Hendley and Blythe sneak onto the field, clobber a German sentry and commandeer a special trainer for a quick escape hop through the nearby Alps. The plane was a little Buker 181 low level observation plane purchased in Hamburg for $325.

After Carrera's crew painted the AT-6s with regulation colors, Sturges watered down the field with fire hoses to simulate early morning. He could not risk his actors in the rickety old Buker so Bob Relyea, an amateur pilot himself, offered to fly the plane for the brief aerial sequences.

The Buker was an unusual plane. Its throttle was located on the left side of the cockpit and in order to start the engine a crank was employed. This presented special problems because Relyea soon found that the plane had a bad habit of stalling in midair. Since one didn't recrank the plane at 6,000 feet, he began to land in some very strange places. "I was beginning to think that when we landed on an airfield, we were lucky," he quipped.

"There is a segment of the film where the Buker is supposedly losing power," he said, "and I was asked to hedgehop with a camera plane alongside to simulate the descent over a line of trees. There was this old farmer plowing a field and he looked up and saw the Buker with it swastikas and out of natural reaction, he threw his rake and almost got me. I always thought that had I been killed, someone would have had to explain to my children that I had been shot down by a rake."

On another occasion, Relyea landed in an innocent looking field that just happened to be the backyard of the local German aviation official. He was flying without a valid license in an obsolete and dangerous aircraft painted with illegal makings and he was placed under arrest until explanations from Sturges engineered his escape.

A decision had not been reached as to who would actually crash the Buker, so the finale with the little plane was postponed. Since both Garner and Pleasance were due to leave Europe (Garner went from *The Great Escape* right into a Doris Day comedy), Sturges decided to shoot the after-action sequence showing the two actors stumbling out of the Buker's wreckage.

"We weren't very smart then," points out Relyea, "because there's a golden rule that you never shoot after-action until you know what the action looks like. When you're dealing with a crashed plane, you don't really know where it's going to land until you see the results of the actual crash. While we were still working on the aerial sequences, we took a mock-up body of the Buker and placed in down on the road below some trees. The actors climbed out of the burning plane and the scene was completed. It was very picturesque and it worked just swell. But I put in the back of my mind that some day I would have to get that shot for John of how the plane got there. It was not something I was looking forward to."

To reconstruct the wartime border between Germany and Switzerland, Sturges worked out a deal with five local farmers for the erection of a fence that eventually grew into a mile and half double barrier.

The motorcycle chase to that border fence begins when Hilts (Steve McQueen), now dressed in the uniform of the tripped motorcyclist, attempts to sneak past a checkpoint near the border.

After tripping up a German motorcyclist, Hilts (Steve McQueen) steals bike and uniform and races for the safety of Switzerland. — The Great Escape (*UA, 1963*).

He is spotted by a guard (stuntman Roy Jensen) and questioned. Since he lacks the proper identification, Hilts kicks the soldier and frantically rides off, only to be followed by several motorcyclists with sidecars.

This particular scene, one of the film's most dramatic, had McQueen take off on one of the camouflaged Triumphs, followed by a sidecar manned by Bud Ekins and Chuck Hayward. The action called for Hilts to cut a corner and scurry across a little foot bridge, while the Germans misjudge the turn and crash through a fence and fall into a gulley.

"It wasn't a breakaway fence," relates Ekins, "but the real thing. And buried beneath the grass was another board which changed the direction of the bike at the last minute, clipping Chuck in the groin. He was thrown to the ground and ended up in the hospital. I was okay although my neck hurt. I fell with the bike and got thrown against the sidecar."

To Sturges' dismay, the German stunt riders hired in Munich could not keep up with hard riding McQueen. They were primarily experienced as highway racers and were out of their element on the dirt roads that crisscrossed the meadowlands.

One morning Sturges was mulling over the problem when he felt a tap on his shoulder. He turned around and was greeted by a fully dressed German soldier with little beer bottle glasses. It was Steve McQueen. Before Sturges could say anything, McQueen said, "Now you know they wouldn't recognize me." And Sturges agreed, "By God, they wouldn't!"

As a result, in several scenes, McQueen rides off as Hilts, the action is stopped, he comes riding back, gets off his bike, changes his clothes, puts on the German uniform and rides over the same ground in pursuit of himself. The sequence worked perfectly, and it wasn't until years later that Sturges revealed that the swift moving German stunt rider was actually McQueen. Comments Sturges, "The Germans had a lot of guts, but they weren't really stuntmen. Curiously enough if you're a real motorcyclist you're not necessarily a good stuntman, because a stuntman knows how to fall off a bike. Whereas a real professional bike rider's whole purpose is to try and stay on the bike. We were lucky to have Steve with us. With exceptional cutting he could have played the entire German Motorcycle Corps."

The most spectacular scene in the film is Hilts' jump for freedom where he negotiates a six-foot barbed wire entanglement. Originally, Sturges wanted Ekins to achieve the necessary height with a wooden ramp, but it was clear that a ramp, even one well camouflaged, was too obvious.

Early in September, while Sturges completed the train and aerial sequences, Ekins, Tim Gibbs and a German special effects technician spent a few hours near the new fence discussing the stunt. They soon discovered a natural wallow that curved down and then upright. Taking the barrier down in one place, they started racing into the wallow to see how high they could actually jump. Gibbs tried it first and jumped the motorcycle six feet across the wallow and two feet off the ground. Retrieving shovels from their utility truck, the trio started digging to created a sharper incline.

Ekins now took the handlebars and raced into the wallow, doubling Gibbs' previous attempt. The digging continued. Steve McQueen arrived and was promptly handed a shovel. Soon, everyone was racing the motorcycle while the special effects man stood by, measuring each jump with a piece of string.

When the digging was completed, the wallow resembled the shape of a jai alai racket. As the motorcycles hit the ditch, the suspension would drop, the bike would hit the incline sharply and simply pop out of the hole. The logistics became so critical that Ekins was digging an inch at a time. By evening the bikes were sailing 40 and 50 feet. They were ready for the cameras.

Far to the north, Robert Relyea was planning an even more critical stunt. After two weeks of careful planning, the special effects crew had determined that there were exactly three ways in which to crash the tiny Buker.

They could put the plane up on a chute, like a ski jump, and glide it in mechanically. This they reasoned would involve a very short entry and zero control and they could end up wrecking the airplane without being sure of a good scene. Or they could

---

Facing page: *To perfect the famed motorcycle jump sequence, practice was essential. Here Steve McQueen shoots out of a carefully designed hollow that gave the motorcycle the required lift. His friend, ace biker Bud Ekins, did the actual on-screen jump.* — The Great Escape *(UA, 1963)*.

After ditching the uniform, Hilts (McQueen) makes for the Swiss border and freedom, in a scene from The Great Escape *(UA, 1963).*

guide the Buker in with wires, which would allow more effective control. However, the entry distance would have been greatly reduced, further inhibiting the plane's velocity at point of impact, and thus the realism of the stunt.

The third choice was obvious: have a stuntman fly the plane into the trees. This way someone could direct the plane up until the moment of impact. Had he been given the choice, Relyea would have definitely eliminated the third alternative as being far too dangerous. Since the after-action had already been shot and there could be no room for error, there was to be no choice.

Bravely resolving that he alone could destroy the Buker (everyone else, including Sturges, thought him crazy), Relyea selected six camera positions and began practicing the run in a nearby field dotted with little flags simulating the distance between his adversaries: the trees.

He was doing well until Reddish asked him to bring up his tail by taxiing a little faster to simulate a landing. While practicing such a maneuver, Relyea crashed into a flag head on. Had it been one of the trees, the engine of the Buker would have had to pass through the cockpit, leaving the pilot with a terribly permanent naval ornament. It was a frightening experience and Relyea considered forgetting the entire sequence.

While he rationalized that model work was prohibitively expensive, the crew prepared the stunt for the next morning. The weather that had remained pleasant enough for motorcycle work suddenly changed for the worse and the next day dawned dark and cloudy. Since the crash could only be filmed in blazing sunshine (it had to be done in one shot and the cameras needed maximum lighting) Relyea was granted a temporary reprieve.

The clouds stood guard over the crash site for two days. As dawn broke on the third day, Relyea's fear was intense. He wife arrived in time to inform him that if he went ahead with the crazy stunt, she would never speak to him again.

The special effects crew prepared the vulnerable little Buker for its appointment with disaster, sawing off the control stick, taking the glass out of the canopy, constructing a special reinforced seat and carefully draining off the excess gasoline. As the Buker was 90 percent wood, a fire crew stood by. Every time Relyea went behind a bush to be sick, he would see the firemen standing by with their buckets of crushed ice. It was enough to drain any man's confidence.

At last, everything was ready. As he revved up the engine, and the crew prepared to disconnect the anchor which held the plane in place, Reddish came running up, climbed onto the wing and shouted above the deafening roar, "Camera five wants to change to a 50mm lens, what do you think?"

Relyea screamed, "I don't care if he puts a coke bottle on it, if I don't go in the next five seconds we're forgetting the whole thing!"

His anchor gone, Relyea cut his flaps, pulled back on the miniature throttle and rolled forward. When halfway across his makeshift runway (actually a cow pasture) he noticed the Buker rolling toward the right tree. He compensated by hitting his right rudder pedal. Fearful that he would accidentally cut power while adjusting his rudder, Relyea rammed the throttle forward and removed his hand, hoping that he could hang on and be able to jab a little rudder at the last minute and avoid the telltale tree.

Removing his hand from the throttle nearly killed him. Hoping to hit the tree at 45 miles an hour he looked down at his indicators, a second before impact, and noticed the Buker pushing 100. It was much too fast.

"I realized how fast I was going, and I had just enough time to hit the left rudder before the plane struck. I involuntarily closed my eyes and felt a terribly slight shudder. And then it was over and I thought, 'that wasn't bad!' I opened my eyes and all I saw was blue sky, which was funny because I expected to be down in the dirt near the road. It then dawned on me that I had hit so hard that I had ripped the Buker's landing gear and wings off and that I was headed towards the Austrian border."

Near the edge of the road, Jack Reddish turned to Mrs. Relyea and said, "Where the hell is he going?"

When Relyea did hit the ground, the force of the crash knocked him unconscious. Seconds later, the four firemen arrived to unstrap him and cover the plane with ice. "They took me to a Munich hospital," Relyea says, "because when I recovered my senses I had a sharp pain in my back. The wet X-rays showed a line down my spinal column so I was sure that I was paralyzed for life. Fortunately, wet x-rays do lie, and I was okay. I had a little trouble for a couple of years, as a long drive would tire me out, but on the whole I survived unscathed."

Ironically, months later, in 1963, after the film's release, Sturges received a letter from a young girl in Canada who complained, "When you make such an expensive film, why do you suddenly get so cheap and make the airplane crash in miniature?"

* * *

Bud Ekins' heart was pounding. Sturges' wrist watch read 2:01. On a little saddleback ridge, John Flynn and Jack Reddish signaled that the cameras were ready. The director raised his arm, signalling Ekins. The crowd around the Chapman crane pushed forward. Steve McQueen leaned against a tire and waited for his "twin" to streak by. The crackle of the Triumph's engine echoed across the meadowland. And then he was off, the streaking illusion of Steve McQueen, blue sweatshirt and dirty beige pants fluttering nervously in the artificial wind.

With considerable ease, Ekins took the Triumph into the jai alai racket wallow, expertly jumping the motorcycle 65 feet, hurtling the six-foot barrier with a foot to spare.

A cheer went up from the crowd of onlookers. The German soldiers whistled their approval, and Steve McQueen leaned over to offer his congratulations. John Sturges simply smiled to Daniel Fapp, and climbed down from the Chapman crane. Spying the catering truck, he remembered he was hungry.

II

The Thin Red Line

Once combat films regained their popularity with postwar audiences, film makers turned from purely battle action exercises to films that explored the psychological motivation of fighting men.

It began in the same year that *Battleground* was released, with films like Stanley Kramer's *Home of the Brave*, which dealt effectively with racial prejudice on a Pacific Island. Through narcosynthesis, a young black Marine overcomes his handicap by reliving the nightmare of prejudice he suffered under combat conditions. *Home of the Brave* was the "sleeper" of 1949 and served to propel the careers of Kramer, director Mark Robson, and writer Carl Foreman, all World War II Veterans.

William Wyler's *The Best Years of Our Lives* (1946) had earlier explored the lives of returning soldiers who found it difficult to make the adjustment from combat to civilian life. There were new films that followed this dramatic success. In director Fred Zinneman's 1950 film *The Men,* a young Marlon Brando tries to readjust to society after a wartime injury makes him a paraplegic.

There were films that treated the "misfits" as a separate distinct class of fighting man. In *The War Lover* (Columbia, 1962), Steve McQueen portrayed Army Air Corps Captain Buzz Rickson, an expert pilot who cannot adjust to life on the ground.

Earlier, in 1953, Columbia Pictures released *From Here to Eternity,* a pre-World War II story that presented three outstanding portraits of soldiers under stress, in this case, during peacetime in Hawaii. Private Robert E. Lee Prewitt (Montgomery Clift), a stubborn bugler, Angelo Maggio (Frank Sinatra), a misfit

116

Italian private, and Milton Warden (Burt Lancaster), a career soldier, all represented the pre-Pearl Harbor professional Army at its rawest. It was an excellent film (an Academy Award winner as best picture of 1953) and it captured the interest as well as the hearts of the audiences of its time.

Along with psychological motivation, there were many films which dealt effectively with stress and its relationship to command and responsibility among wartime officers. In *The Mountain Road* (1960), an inexperienced demolitions officer (James Stewart) misuses his responsibility and precipitates a massacre on a mountain road in East China in 1944.

In *Run Silent, Run Deep* (1958), a submarine commander (Clark Gable) drives his crew relentlessly with a "Moby Dick" obsession to battle a Japanese destroyer. In producer Otto Preminger's *In Harm's Way*, (1965), a naval commander (Kirk Douglas) survives the humiliating death of his wife, but forever harbors a mistrust for all women. Once he rapes a young girl, losing the respect of his only friend (John Wayne), he virtually commits suicide by attacking a Japanese battle fleet single-handedly.

In releasing films of this type, American film makers were able to lend to the combat film a new sophistication that was in keeping with Hollywood's overall maturity. The big blockbuster war picture that offered only action and adventure was no longer the darling of the critics or the audiences. The innocence of the 1940's was gone and the interest in war had taken on a new perspective.

RKO president Howard Hughes' decision to sell Dore Schary's *Battleground* project to MGM in the summer of 1948 was based on his conviction that postwar audiences were far more interested in aerial adventures than slow moving infantry combat.

However prejudiced his decision seemed at the time (Hughes was already famous as an aircraft manufacturer and expert pilot), it was based on a gut feeling that the popularity of the Air Force in a series of post-World War I adventure dramas could be rekindled. Back in 1931, when war films were a risky venture, Hughes had produced his highly successful film, *Hell's Angels*. Two decades later, under similiar conditions, it seemed reasonable that such fare could repeat its success.

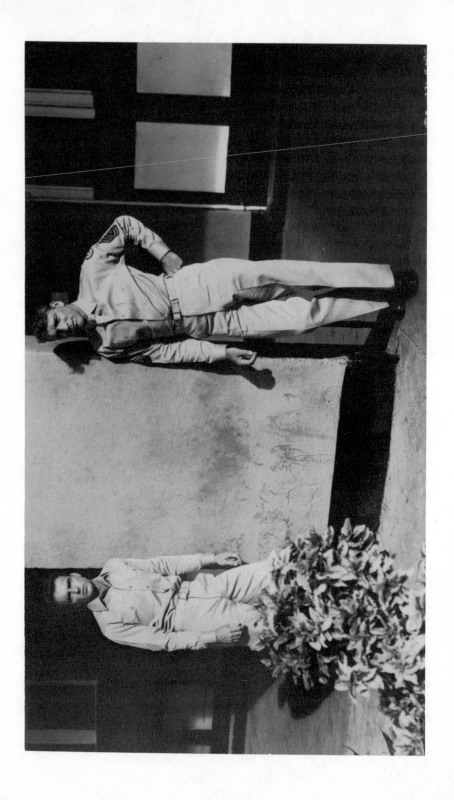

*Shirley Ann Field tells Steve McQueen, who has forced his way into her flat,
"You don't know how to love, you only know how to hate," in this scene from*
The War Lover *(Columbia, 1962).*

Hell's Angels and the earlier *Wings* (1927) sparked the big
World War I aviation cycle that continued in various forms until
the end of World War II. Most of the air sagas of this period offered the very elements of flight extolled by Howard Hughes:
escapist adventure, airborne romance, and daredevil action. For
two decades (1919-1939), the airplane was to symbolize an escape
from the Depression. Various aspects of flying were featured in almost every film. A mechanical fascination, the airplane offered high
adventure that lifted the audiences out of their spiritual depression.

Facing page: *The stars of* From Here to Eternity *(Columbia, 1953) were Montgomery Clift, left, playing loner Robert E. Lee Pruitt, who refused to box for his
company and pays the price, and Burt Lancaster as Sergeant Warden, who commands a platoon of professional soldiers in prewar Pearl Harbor.*

But there were no exceptions. *The Dawn Patrol,* based on a story by Howard Hawks and John Monk Saunders and released by Warner Brothers in 1938, was one of the only films of its time to explore a deeper meaning. Unfortunately, its symbolic warning was soon forgotten in the rush to a new war.

The film stars Errol Flynn and David Niven and tells the story of the 59th Squadron of the British Flying Corps fighting in France during World War I when the superior German Air Force was sweeping the British from the skies. Using obsolete planes and equipment, the unit valiantly tries to turn the tide, ultimately paying a heavy price in human life.

Although the aerial sequences were impressive in terms of realism, the film emphasized the low key atmosphere at the aerodrome. Many scenes took place in the club bar where the names of downed airmen were erased from a blackboard and *Poor Butterfly* was played repeatedly on a small record player. An air of doomed camaraderie prevailed.

Released one year before Germany's invasion of Poland and the start of World War II, *The Dawn Patrol* was one of the last of the aerial anti-war films. For the American isolationists, it was their high water mark. After Pearl Harbor and the London Blitz, pacifism became obsolete. Whatever the cost, America must win the war. Hollywood went with the winner.

During the war, the true sacrifice of the airman depicted in films like *The Dawn Patrol* was seldom dramatized. Aerial warfare retained a distinct individualism and sense of adventure on the screen, while, in reality, military aviation had become more destructive than ever. Biplane chivalry had been buried in the rubble of Warsaw and Coventry. Individuality of the Eddie Rickenbacker variety had faded, crushed beneath the sheer magnitude of the air war.

Aerial combat was now a massive undertaking fought by thousands. The punitive squadron attack so costly during the First World War had been replaced by new tactics like the group saturation raid. To blacken the sky with aircraft was no longer an idle boast as wings and air divisions became common flying units, amassing hundreds and thousands of bombers at once. Attended by wailing air raid sirens, crumbling cities, and homeless refugees, the airplane had become a symbol of aerial death.

5

A Change of Emphasis

If you stood suspended in space above a B-17 Flying Fortress you could visualize an imaginary clock. The nose of the plane would be at 12 o'clock, the tail at 6, the wings at 3 and 9. The clock was the key to the bomber's aerial defense. In describing the angle of an attacking German fighter, the pilot and the crew would pinpoint their direction by yelling out a time on the clock.

It wasn't long before the Germans realized that their best bet was to attack a Fortress from a position at 12 o'clock and high. Given the defensive weakness of the B-17's nose and the tremendous closing velocity which propelled fighter and bomber towards each other at a combined speed of over 800 miles an hour, an Me-109 or FW-190 (Germany's principle day fighters) could seriously damage a B-17 without commiting suicide. The term "twelve o'clock high" was thus considered a synonym, among airmen, for potential danger. It was also to be the title of a very important combat film of the late 1940's.

Released at the same time as *Battleground* and *Home of the Brave, Twelve O'Clock High* was Darryl F. Zanuck's entry in the 1948-49 combat film revival. While Howard Hughes fussed and fretted over *Battleground*, Zanuck produced the depressing story of the 8th Air Force's early days as an understrength combat unit. A classic study of the meaning of command and the danger of stress, the film returned to the spirit of *The Dawn Patrol*, placing character interaction on the ground consistently above combat spectacle in the air. Moreover, *Twelve O'Clock High* was the product of two Air Force officers who, like Robert Pirosh, were interested in putting the remembrances of times past on film for the world to see.

Col. Beirne Lay, Jr., commander of the 487th Bomb Wing (as he looked in March 1944) and coauthor of Twelve O'Clock High.

In the summer of 1931, the United States had no Air Force. Hampered by a severely restricted budget, the infant Army Air Corps was struggling for existance. Its fate varied from year to year. A generous appropriation from the War Department (highly uncommon) meant more cadets, newer planes and better facilities, while a minuscule appropriation (the rule during the Depression) meant far less of everything.

Fortunately for Yale graduate Beirne Lay, Jr., he entered the Air Corps during an upswing. The combined pressure applied to the General Staff by young officers like Carl Spaatz, Henry Arnold and George Kenney was having an effect. For the moment, there were openings for those whose motto would be "I Wanted Wings!"

Lay headed south that June to Randolph Field, Texas, for his first eight months of basic training. While headlines spoke of Wiley Post and his trip around the world in a plane named *Winnie Mae*, the Ivy Leaguer turned pilot was encountering his own adventures.

At Randolph, and later at nearby Kelly Field where he spent four months in the bombardment section flying ancient Keystone bombers, Lay gained the firsthand experiences about which he chose to write.

Almost a decade before he coauthored *Twelve O'Clock High* with screenwriter Sy Bartlett, Lay was to write his first book, appropriately entitled, *I Wanted Wings!* Paramount Pictures producer Arthur Hornblow, Jr., later purchased the rights to the book and Lay was brought to Hollywood to write his first screenplay. Directed by Mitchel Leisen and released shortly before Pearl Harbor in 1941, the film version of Lay's novel isolated a segment of the great American military buildup by following three air cadets through cadet training.

Between 1933 and 1938 Lay served several tours of active duty at Langley Field, Virginia. Since Air Corps appropriations were so variable, he would alternate at times between inactive reserve and active status. Shortly after the German invasion of Poland on September 1, 1939, Lay was assigned to Ontario Field, California, as a primary flight training instructor. Three months later he was summoned to Air Corps Headquarters in Washington. Colonel Ira Eaker had sent for him. Lay found himself, among other duties, assigned to Staff as Henry "Hap" Arnold's speech writer. Waiting for a transfer to London and observer status, Lay was still in better shape than his future partner, Sy Bartlett.

Forever fascinated by flying and air power, Bartlett had been thrown in the Signal Corps, attached to Colonel Schlossberg's Army Pictorial Service. There it was felt he could use his film background to contribute a great deal to the new breed of training films. But Sy wanted to fly, or at least he wanted to be attached to a flying unit. A war was coming and the last thing he wanted to do was edit training documentaries.

It was Beirne Lay who brought about Bartlett's transfer into the Air Corps. Although the two were strangers, Bartlett know of Lay's work on *I Wanted Wings*. When orders transferred Bartlett to the Signal Corps Center in Washington, he asked his friend Arthur Hornblow, Jr., to set up a meeting.

As a member of Colonel Eaker's staff, First Lieutenant Lay was on good terms with many of the Air Corps' senior officers. The two writers became close friends and it was not long before Captain Bartlett was introduced to General Walter Weaver, Chief of the Air Corps. Through Weaver, he met Carl Spaatz, who would soon command the American Air Forces in Europe.

"Tooey" Spaatz had just returned from England where he had been observing the Royal Air Force in combat. While the United States was sending bombers and destroyers to England as part of Lend-Lease, the rapidly growing Army Air Corps was keeping a weary eye fixed on the European Air War through a close liaison with RAF Bomber Command.

On his return, General Spaatz began to record his observations. He also organized a small staff, the nucleus of which later became the United States Army Air Force. Sy Bartlett joined Spaatz's staff as the General's aide.

Of the two writers, Lay, now a captain, was the first to be ordered overseas. Eaker, who like Spaatz, had served as a special observer with the RAF in 1941, returned the following year with the rank of brigadier general and orders to set up the 8th Bomber Command. An integral part of the General's seven-man advanced detachment, Lay arrived in war torn London on February 20, 1942.

His was an interesting tour of duty. When Eaker released him from his staff assignment with the 8th Air Force as chief of its Film Unit, Lay began training on the newly arrived B-17's. He flew nine bombing missions with the "Bloody 100th" Bomb Group, including the disastrous raid on the Regensberg fighter plane factory in Germany. In late 1943, he was ordered stateside for advanced training on the B-24 "Liberator," an American heavy bomber then being put into mass production.

Barely six months later, Lay was flying again, this time as commanding officer of the 487th Bombardment Group, which he led overseas from Alamogordo, New Mexico, in March 1944. On May 11 of that year the 487th was alerted for a strike against Chaumont, a railroad marshaling yard in Eastern France. About 120 miles southeast of Paris, Lay's command ship was struck by antiaircraft fire and shot down. Colonel Lay parachuted safely into occupied France and spent the next three months behind enemy lines, evading capture with the help of the French Underground.

Sy Bartlett had arrived in London on June 3, 1942. He quickly disengaged himself from Spaatz's staff and transferred into the Operational Intelligence Section of the 8th Bomber Command.

While Eaker's group prepared for their first raids, Bartlett observed the British, at times flying as an observer with the "Lancaster Bunch." It was during this association with British Bomber Command that Bartlett stumbled across "RT-Intercepts," a secret RAF operation that could be a plus for U.S. bomber defense.

Since 1940, English radar stations had been monitoring the Luftwaffe's radio traffic. Soon after its first missions, the RAF was receiving regular reports on German fighter reaction to their raids. At a secret communications complex in Gloucester, British military Intelligence (MI-6) had trained German speaking English girls to monitor the Luftwaffe radio transmissions. Within weeks, the girls became familiar with the enemy pilots, instantly recognizing their peculiar "chatter."

When a British strike was launched, the tactical deployment of key German fighters units was observed and catalogued. These reports were extremely valuable. With the constant stream of information flowing into their planning rooms, British Bomber Command was able to counter the effective German Fighter defense and thus neturalize the latter's ability to break up RAF bomber formations.

Still, the British did all of their bombing at night, a time when German fighter strength was minimal. It was the American Air Forces that had opted for precision daylight bombing. Fighters would thus be a far more formidable threat to the Americans. Bartlett wanted those RT-Intercepts for Spaatz. If there was a way to save American lives, he meant to have it.

Bartlett's campaign to win for the Americans the vital information eventually proved successful. (The program later became an important ingredient in the novel: Patricia Mallory, a pretty young Wren officer who falls in love with General Savage, works in the underground complex at Gloucester, and tries to sell the General on the program's importance to the American Air Force).

As chief officer in charge of RT-Intercepts, Bartlett left Pinetree (8th Air Force Headquarters at Wycombe Down) regularly, to brief the front line groups commanders. He especially liked to visit Colonel Frank Armstrong, the commander of the 306th Bombardment Group at Thurleigh Field. Armstrong, who had lead the first ten missions against the Germans, was considered one of the Air Corps' most outstanding combat leaders. Beirne Lay, Jr., had known him before the war at Barksdale Field in Louisiana when the latter commanded one of the Air Corps squadrons flying A-3 attack planes.

It was at Thurleigh while visiting with Armstrong, that Lay and Bartlett began to discuss the possibility of writing an intimate narrative about the 8th Air Force.

It was to be their last wartime meeting. Group Commander Lay had just returned from France, via the Underground, and was headed home. Air Force regulations prevented his return to a combat unit, not only for his own protection should he be shot down again, but for the protection of his French Underground contacts. Lay's escape through enemy lines would produce a later book appropriately entitled, *I've Had It!*

At Thurleigh Field, Bartlett told Lay, "You know, when this war ends, people are going to forget what happened here. They won't care anymore. To prevent that from happening, you and I are going to write a novel about the Air Corps. It will take

General Frank Armstrong, center (prototype for the Gregory Peck "Frank Savage" role), commander of a B-29 bombardment group in the Pacific, and Twelve O'Clock High coauthor Sy Bartlett (left), with war correspondent Richard Tregaskis.

place at a solitary field like this one and we'll have a central character like Frank Armstrong.

"And," he continued, "when we finish the novel, we'll write
a screenplay. It will be the best war film ever. With your combat
experience and my inside knowledge of the command structure, we
can write this thing from a unique point of view."

Bartlett remained in the Tactical Section of the 8th Air Force
until the war in Europe ended. After a brief tour of duty with a
B-29 training command, he joined Brig. Gen. Armstrong's staff
and headed for the Pacific where the war had still to be won.

Before Hiroshima and Nagasaki brought the Second World
War to a close, Colonel Bartlett flew with the 315th Combat
Wing. Aptly tagged the "Gypsy Rose Lee Unit," Bartlett's aircraft
were stripped of all armament in favor of a huge bomb load.

Twelve O'Clock High was born as a novel on a sunny day in
the spring of 1946. The two Air Force officers were once more
civilians, Lay as an active free lance writer, Bartlett a contract
screenwriter at 20th Century-Fox. Lay had invited his friend to
Santa Barbara for a pleasant day of recollection, but Bartlett was
interested in a more constructive approach to the past. He still
wanted to write the definitive Air Force novel. Lay immediately
tried to sidestep the issue.

He told Bartlett, "I've been giving it a lot of thought, and it
seems to me that it's too soon after the war for such a project.
Sure, we could publish a book, but you know the real money is in a
film. The time just isn't right. People are tired of war films."

"You're right," replied Bartlett, "but forget about the film
possibilities for now. Let's write the novel. I know Hollywood,
when we finish the book, I guarantee we'll have no problem selling
the film rights." He concluded by appealing to Lay's conscience.
There was no way they could let people forget men like Armstrong
or fields like Thurleigh Aerodrome. It was their responsibility to
let people know.

That same day, they outlined their main character, a
brigadier general named Frank Savage, a composite of generals
Armstrong and Curtis Lemay, the former contributing his good
looks, a rugged disposition and a blend of masterfully inspired
leadership, the latter a sense of discipline that would lend Savage
his over-powering sense of mission.

Brig. Gen. Savage would command the mythical 918th Bombardment Group, a numerical designation arrived at by Lay, who merely multiplied Armstrong's own 306th Group by three. Bomber command headquarters retained its code name, Pinetree. Thurleigh Aerodrome was changed to Archbury.

In the novel, an Air Corps Colonel named Keith Davenport, the 918th's original commanding officer, sacrifices discipline and becomes overly identified with his men, ultimately losing his sense of command and strategic purpose. General Savage leaves his position at Pinetree to assume command of Davenport's jinxed Bombardment Group.

These events were based entirely on fact. Only five weeks after Armstrong left his own 97th Group to assume a staff position, he was asked to relieve "Chip" Overacker, commander of the 306th at Thurleigh.

Sy Bartlett had accompanied the General to Thurleigh on that fateful morning. "When we drove through the gate," he recalled, "past the sentry without being challenged, I knew it was going to be one of those days. Frank blew his stack. It was only the beginning. Thurleigh was a mess. The officers were drunk. All over the base military protocol and discipline were completely lax. There was no pride whatsoever. Frank found it appalling."

In addition to formulating the basic plot, each writer contributed his own brand of expertise. Bartlett gave *Twelve O'Clock High* its excellent sense of dramatic structure, drawing on his long experience as a screenwriter. His RT-Intercept program was a natural addition to the novel, as was the love affair between Wren officer Patricia Mallory and Savage.

Beirne Lay, Jr., contributed a sense of realism and the actual experience of command responsibility as a pilot. As a bomb group commander, he spoke from experience. On the Regensberg/Schweinfurt raid, one of the war's most hazardous, he had flown as an observer with the 100th Bombardment Group. After the raid, General Curtis Lemay had asked him to submit a report on the mission. It was later published almost verbatim in the Saturday Evening Post. The bare facts needed no embellishment.

Like Robert Pirosh, Lay experienced war at first hand and possessed the unique writing talent of lucid interpretation. He didn't bog his writing down in tactics and strategy, names and

places. He wrote with a certain honest feeling that more effectively conveyed the reality of the air war. Combining this talent with Bartlett's behind the scenes knowledge made *Twelve O'Clock High* the classic flying novel of World War II.

Months before it was published, in the winter of 1946-47, Bartlett had interested Fox producer Louis D. Lighton, a former story editor under David O. Selznick at MGM, in the project, and Lighton in turn began a personal campaign to win over Darryl Zanuck. It was no easy task. War films remained a cool topic at the boxoffice.

Fortunately, Lighton was not the only interested producer. Bartlett's friend, director William Wyler, had expressed enthusiasm from the beginning. It was only natural. Wyler himself was an Air Force veteran, and as commander of a combat camera unit, had produced one of the war's finest aerial documentaries, *The Memphis Belle*, a film about a B-17's 25th mission and a ticket home.

As fate would have it, it was Beirne Lay, Jr., who had greeted Wyler when he arrived in London in mid-1942. Eaker had ordered him to take temporary charge of the director's camera unit, get the men quartered and organize equipment and basic traning for the combat photographers.

Against orders, Wyler later flew as a waist gunner, camera in hand, on several raids (one, during which he lost most of his hearing when the plane he was in was hit by antiaircraft), much to the chagrin of Lay who had been ordered by Eaker to ground Wyler. The Nazis, it turns out, had put a big price on the head of Wyler, who had directed *Mrs. Miniver*.

"Whatever his other qualities, he had enormous guts," Lay recalled. "This wasn't easy. Someone on a set might think he was a sonofabitch or a sadist because he wanted twenty takes of a scene, but here in aerial combat, was the acid test. With his own skin on the line, he went out there and took the pictures he wanted."

Bartlett, Lay and Wyler resumed their friendship in

Facing page: *"How do I address you?" snaps General Frank Savage (Gregory Peck) to Sergeant McIlhenny (Robert Arthur) upon first arriving to take command of a base in disciplinary shambles.* — Twelve O'Clock High *(20th Century-Fox, 1949).*

Hollywood four years later. A bidding war soon erupted between Wyler at Paramount Pictures and Lighton at Fox. Financially, such a competition was a windfall for the writers. Their agent quickly upped the novel's price to a whopping (for its time) $100,000. The critical factor was Zanuck, who had remained lukewarm to the project until Wyler entered the fray. He had great respect for the boxoffice success of Wyler's latest film, *The Best Years of Our Lives*. With that in mind he authorized Lighton to outbid Wyler and win *Twelve O'Clock High* for 20th Century-Fox.

In going over the novel with the writers, prior to the writing of the screenplay, Bud Lighton found several sub themes, and while they enhanced the book's realism, they would only create confusion in a motion picture. Lighton had already decided that the subordinate themes would have to go, so the writers began to trim their book. As Selznick's story editor, Lighton had learned the importance of a tightly written script, and with Zanuck's key interest in the project, his writers weren't going to get carried away with a long overproduced screenplay.

"You can have only one principle theme," Lighton told Bartlett, "if Savage is your main character, then we have to eliminate some of the other material, you can't have everything." Primary among these crosscurrents was the bitter behind the scenes rivalry at Pinetree. This was Bartlett's arena. The command structure at 8th Air Force headquarters resembled the batting order on a major league baseball team. When an officer proved inefficient, he was bounced back to the minors, which in Air Force jargon was a stateside training command. Personal relationships were always to be sacrificed for the strategic good.

Bartlett, while working in operational intelligence, discovered that Spaatz and Arnold frequently surrounded themselves with a group of prewar flying buddies who were neither effective leaders nor competent tacticians.

In the novel, Bartlett put these conflicts to work. Jealousy pervaded the atmosphere of Pinetree. Savage's superiors continually attempt to send him back to the States. Effective leader-

---

Facing page: *Gen. Savage (Gregory Peck) telephones headquarters while Col. Keith Davenport (Gary Merrill, left) and Major Harvey Stovall (Dean Jagger) look on.* — Twelve O'Clock High *(20th Century-Fox, 1949).*

The Waiting game at Archbury. Savage (Peck) and Stovall (Jagger) await the return of the B-17 Group. Dean Jagger's part as the aging retread won him the supporting Oscar for 1949. — Twelve O'Clock High (20th Century-Fox, 1949).

ship was often canceled out as one superior after another tried to hamper the General's mission. This was strong material, but it watered down the impact of the main theme. In Lighton's eyes, the Pinetree rivalry was unnecessary. With a painful wince from Bartlett, it was eliminated.

The novel's love story was yet another victim. "However natural it is to have Wren officer Mallory skulking about," Lighton told Lay, "it's damn distracting. Here we're trying to build Savage into a rock of Gibraltar, and he has this convenient release."

Lay fought for Mallory, arguing that it was this very

release that contributed to Savage's eventual collapse. Lay told Lighton, "You get used to the pressure because it remains steady. Sometimes it's almost unbearable, but you take it. Remember what Savage said at his first briefing at Archbury. 'Write yourself off. Tell yourself you're already dead. Once you accept that fact it will be easier to fly those missions.' That was his philosophy. He had already written himself off. But something happened when he met Patricia Mallory. Suddenly he had a release, someone to think about. He was no longer effectively isolated. It was the kind of distraction that would eventually destroy him."

Lighton accepted Lay's reasoning, but when the script went forty pages over schedule, the love story was doomed. Patricia Mallory and the RT-Intercept Program became the novel's final casualties. Although taskmaster Lighton continued trimming the novel and establishing a powerful overriding theme, he concurrently stretched the remaining scenes with reams of dialogue. Work eventually ground to a halt. A conflict had developed in the crucial confrontation between Savage and playboy Officer Ben Gately.

Zanuck was furious. In the subdued atmosphere of depressing Archbury, *Twelve O'Clock High* characters had become nonstop chatterboxes. Symbolism had disappeared like a disabled B-17. Lighton was fired from the project and *Twelve O'Clock High* was placed on Zanuck's "what the hell do we do with it now?" shelf.

For six months (March to September 1948) the project stagnated. Zanuck and the writers could not agree on the revisions. Aside from the ponderous dialogue, Bartlett agreed with his partner and later informed Zanuck that the impasse centered on the crucial hospital confrontation between Savage and a wounded Gately.

In the novel, Gately, Davenport's playboy chief air executive, is busted to airplane commander when Savage takes a dim view of his leisurely military attitude. "You're a coward and a disgrace to this whole outfit," the enraged Savage tells him. To complete the humiliation, Gately is placed in command of "The Leper Colony," a lone B-17 crewed by nine other misfits.

The antagonism between the officers is maintained to the very end of the novel when Savage discovers a new side to the man he once called coward. The awakening occurs in the Archbury

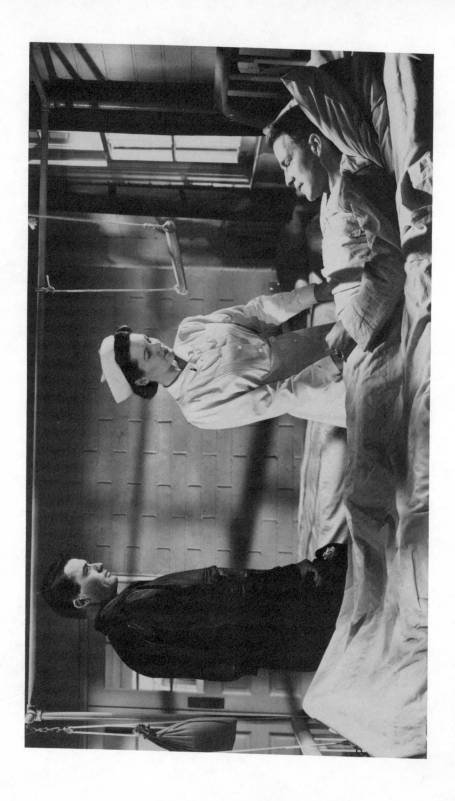

hospital. Through Doc Kaiser, Savage learns that Gately is in traction, suffering from a painful spinal fracture caused by his ditching in the English Channel on a previous mission. Despite excruciating pain, Gately continued to fly "The Leper Colony" on the next three raids.

"It was a very awkward situation for both men," says Bartlett, "as there is still this great tension between them. Savage sits quietly at Gately's side, unable to articulate his feelings, the latter equally powerless to accept favors from the man who has treated him so roughly."

Bartlett thought the confrontation should end in stalemate. Lay disagreed, claiming that it was time the tension between the two men eased. Although he agreed that an outright commendation was out of character, Lay felt Savage should somehow communicate his regard for the officer's perseverance and that Gately should accept the reevaluation.

It was a touching scene. Savage's hard shell was finally cracking, the question was how much? Eventually the two writers compromised. Both officers would retain their unyielding positions in person, but once outside the hospital, Savage would praise the fallen airman within earshot of his window. Gately accepts the praise with a smile, and the conflict is resolved. In the novel, it was an effective solution.

It is important to remember that the Gately and Savage rivalry was only one of the novel's dramatic conflicts. While the change in emphasis in the hospital scene was important, it was not critical to the outcome of the book. The screenplay, however, presented a whole new series of problems.

Lighton had quickly eliminated all of the subsidiary conflicts, making Savage's character transformation, from "rock of Gibraltar" to caring individual, the film's primary theme. Thus, the final confrontation with Gately was crucial to the script. In the film's final scene, Gately would lead the squadron in Savage's absence. The man who was branded a coward returns to base with all

---

Facing page: *Huge Marlowe shines in the role of playboy Ben Gately who gains the respect of Gen. Savage (Peck, left) only after flying several missions in pain from a spinal injury. Joyce Mackenzie portrays the nurse.* — Twelve O'Clock High *(20th Century-Fox, 1949).*

but two aircraft. It was impossible to work the novel's compromise into the script. An overheard conversation, along with a smile were cinematically ineffective. Zanuck also wanted the conflict to simmer until Gately finally proves himself.

In late September 1948, Bartlett, newly arrived director Henry King and Zanuck met in Palm Springs to dicuss a suitable ending. It was clear to all that Savage could never outwardly express his feelings to Gately. It was too far out of character. For Savage to remain withdrawn was more in keeping with his disposition.

It was Sy Bartlett's solution that prevented another impasse and got *Twelve O'Clock High* moving again. He told Zanuck, "Darryl, let's bring in a third party, a nurse. We'll keep the conversation between the two men low key, no giving, no receiving. Then Savage will leave and the nurse will come in and inform Gately, 'Colonel, I've been informed that you're a special case'."

It was a brilliant solution to a knotty problem. Who can forget the tears in Hugh Marlowe's (Gately's) eyes when he hears the nurse. Zanuck took one look at Bartlett then turned to King and said, "Start scouting for locations."

Henry King was one of Zanuck's favorite directors. He was also the movie industry's acknowledged aviation expert. In a space of 25 years, he had logged over one million air miles in his own plane. Combining his interest in flying with his work in film, King was the first Hollywood director to search out locations by plane.

Says King, "Most of *Twelve O'Clock High*'s exteriors were shot at Eglin Field in Florida. It's a tremendous field but hard to get to unless you're flying there. I had Zanuck charter a DC-6, which carried 96 people, and I shipped four tons of equipment by another plane. Thus, a cast of 60 and a crew of 40 were able to leave Hollywood in the morning, unload in Florida in the afternoon and begin shooting the next morning.

"When shooting was completed, I flew my private plane to Big Springs, Texas, stayed overnight and then went on to Hollywood the next day. Meanwhile, a DC-6 took off from Eglin at 9:00 a.m. with the crew and cast and checked into the Westwood studio at 4:30 p.m. Then, after a good night's rest at home, everybody was ready to start work the next morning.

"If this whole setup had been set up by train, at least ten

days would have been lost in travel and even then you would not have a fresh cast ready to start work the next day. Plane travel has cut down to one week on an average what would have taken one month to locate under older methods."

Henry King was also an Air Force veteran who served two years active duty with the Ferry Command, the Gulf of Mexico Submarine Patrol, and as liaison with the Mexican Air Force which, during World War II, guarded the strategic Tampico and Hermosillo oilfields. His contacts with U.S. Army Air Force Headquarters served him well once Zanuck assigned him to *Twelve O'Clock High*.

Four grueling months in Italy filming *Prince of Foxes* had done little to weather King. Ten minutes after his first talk with Zanuck, King was in touch with 20th Century-Fox's chief art director Lyle Wheeler. Through Wheeler, he discovered that former producer Lighton had picked Santa Maria, California, for the film's primary location. With misgivings, King flew north in his private plane with newly assigned art director Maurice Ransford. His premonitions were confirmed. Santa Maria, itself, was level, but the small agricultural community was surrounded by round hillocks and volcanic formations. Rural England it wasn't.

With Zanuck's authorization, King left for the East Coast. In New Jersey, he stopped off at McGuire Air Force Base which proved equally unsuitable. Despite its alluring complement of 11 functioning B-17's, McGuire was structurally too complex to resemble tiny Archbury. A camouflage job was impossible.

After securing Pentagon cooperation in Washington, King went south toward big Eglin Field in Florida. On the way, he picked up Colonel John De Russy at the Army War College in Montgomery, Alabama. De Russy, former commander of the 305th Bombardment Group, left his teaching job to become the film's principle technical advisor.

At Eglin, King resumed his wartime friendship with General Hoyt S. Vandenberg, former commander of the U.S. Ninth Air Force. Vandenberg cheerfully gave the director carte blanche at Eglin.

Ransford and Sy Bartlett were then summoned east to coordinate production plans. While the art director measured the field and estimated production costs, Bartlett underwent a concen-

Unable to take command of his ship, Gen. Savage (Peck) heads for a complete mental collapse. Here he is restrained by Major Stovall (Jagger) and Col. Davenport (Merrill, hidden). — Twelve O'Clock High *(20th Century-Fox, 1949).*

trated 63 hour *tête-à-tête* with King. The topic was script revisions. Lighton's dialogue was being dumped like a cargo of bombs.

After that whirlwind effort, Bartlett returned to Hollywood to transcribe his notes and prepare the final shooting script. King soon followed. The script was mimeographed and sent directly to Zanuck. On January 24, 1949, King's birthday, the director received a phone call from the studio. It was Zanuck. "Henry, it's the best script I've ever read. Happy birthday!"

Two days later, Zanuck signed contract player Gregory Peck to portray General Savage. For Peck and King, it was the beginning of a relationship that accounted for four more successful films: *The Gun Fighter* (1950), *David and Bathsheba* (1951), *The Snows of Kilimanjaro* (1952), and *Beloved Infidel* (1959).

Two other contract players, Gary Merrill and Hugh Marlowe, were signed to play Davenport and Gately, respectively.

Tall, lanky Peck (as a priest, he had captivated Zanuck in *Keys to the Kingdom* in 1943) rose above his gentle personality to give perhaps the finest portrayal of his career, aided by a fine shooting script created by Messers. Bartlett and Lay.

Further helping the production was Zanuck's signing of bald Dean Jagger to play the crucial role of Major Harvey Stovall, the film's most symbolic character. Stovall is the film's conscience, a storyteller through whom we see Archbury's transformation.

Stovall fights his war from behind a desk. While he understands the long term strategies, the logistics, the complications of modern war, his war is with a daily load of paperwork. Life at Archbury retains a human quality for him. He is surrounded by friends. Death becomes a swift moving cloud.

"You get used to the tension," Lay had said early on to Lighton, and it is through Stovall that we understand what he meant. It is also through Stovall that we see Savage change. As much a sounding board as an intermediary with the rest of Archbury, Stovall also becomes the General's self-styled lawyer.

"I'm a retread," he tells the General, "a mud merchant from World War One. I guess when I came over here they felt that I could only command a desk. But I'm a lawyer by profession, General. When I came to Archbury, I took on my biggest client, the 918th Bombardment Group. And, by God, I want to see it win its case at all costs." Stovall's perseverance is a constant reminder to Savage that however mechanistic war has become, it is still waged with human blood.

That Stovall is a retread merely emphasized the fact that two former Air Force officers, turned writers, were telling the story. Like that of *The Dawn Patrol* twenty years earlier, the story of *Twelve O'Clock High* is told from the ground's point of view. It is the daily reactions of men like Stovall who wait for the planes to come back that count. Had the writers endowed fighting characters like Savage or pilot Jesse Bishop with the Major's insights, the film would have forfeited its unique point of view.

The film, as well as the book, begins with a great deal of this symbolism. One year after the war, Harvey Stovall, civilian, discovers a slightly cracked Toby Mug in the window of a south

London haberdashery. It is the very same mug that once graced the mantlepiece of the Archbury Officer's Club.

"Where did you get this?" he asks excitedly of the proprietor. "Why, at Archbury sir."

For Stovall, the Toby unlocks a door to the recent past. Traveling by train, motor car, and then by bicycle, he once again visits Archbury. He strolls across the deserted concrete air strip, now covered with weeds and disinterested cows. And in the background he begins to hear voices.

They sing to him: "Bless them all, Bless them all, The long and the short and the tall...." He scans the field. Atop a decaying control tower, a battered windsock hangs lifelessly.

Then, abruptly, the air is filled with the sound of engines. The weeds are blown backwards by a burst of agitated air. The wind sock comes to life with an energy of its own. Time disappears. It is World War II once more.

6

The Great Adventure

The curtain falls away, the screen goes light and a solitary scavenger bird appears, flapping its wings gracefully as it soars upward into the soft pale blue sky. Evocative of freedom, it has all the time in the world to go about its business. Circling, searching for prey, it appears almost bored with its existence, oblivious to all that is happening around it. And there is a great deal, for this is 1943, and, below, Siam has been overrun and occupied by the Japanese Imperial Army.

Below lies the jungle, a vast entangling carpet of steamy foliage, alive with the sounds of living things, birds, insects, creatures of the land and water. The camera pans through this cacophony, waiting, wondering what will happen next. And then beyond the rot, the untouched, unyielding mass of vegetation that one can almost smell on screen, comes the sound of man.

It is a metallic retort, an alien presence in this atmosphere. But the sound is unmistakable. It is the whistle of a train, a Japanese train moving on crudely lain tracks. There are sentries on the train, holding their rifles lazily, soldiers in a visual sense only. There is no thought of human warfare in this jungle, for the only enemy is a common one—nature. In any case, they are not worried; they are herding only the beaten survivors of the Singapore fiasco.

The train stops and a battalion of British prisoners disembarks. Shorn of its battle flags and insignia, it is a military unit in name only. Physically, the men are a ragged lot with torn uniforms, and skeletal figures, bruised bodies with open sores. Many of them limp and some are carried on stretchers by their comrades. It appears to be another version of the Bataan Death March.

But there is something else here, something otherworldly,

143

something that cannot be seen, but felt. These men move purposefully. They have determination. They are not straggling along, but moving. It is a long way from the parade ground in Singapore, but this British battalion under the command of Lt. Col. L. Nicholson is a unit with spirit. Nicholson himself strides forward with a swagger stick, his chest thrown out, a symbol to his men, the defiant symbol of the British lion in captivity. His battalion is going to survive at all costs, even in this godforsaken jungle on the banks of the River Kwai.

The opening sequence to the 1957 film, *The Bridge on the River Kwai*, is a beautifully engineered example of *cinéma vérité*. There is no air of phony stage theatrics and there are no sound stage limitations. The jungle rot is the real thing, as is the scavenger bird, the Japanese train and the torn British uniforms. Together they tell a story, a visual one that complements well the written word based on French author Pierre Boulle's novel.

Director David Lean's use of the outdoor locations to give the film its constant atmosphere of reality, works almost effortlessly as if nature, herself, had been painted and arranged carefully by an air director who simultaneously coordinated the noise of the jungle with a sound effects editor.

The film was to be a trend setter. In abandoning the sound stages for realistic background, this 1957 blockbuster initiated a general trend in Hollywood that brought back great numbers of the public into motion picture theaters after they had abandoned them in favor of television.

Soon, outdoor films were dazzling audiences with their careful blend of action and eye filling spectacle. It was the age of the road show, and movies suddenly became special events. Films like *The Ten Commandments, Around the World in Eighty Days, Ben Hur, El Cid,* and *The Sound of Music* lured families away from their little boxes and into movie houses in record numbers, replenishing the coffers of a badly sagging industry.

Although the "big event" film was as old as Hollywood itself (*The Birth of a Nation* was the first in a subgenre of spectacular films later produced by such as David O. Selznick, whose *Gone with the Wind* may be Hollywood's most famous film, and Cecil B. De Mille, whose name became a synonym for epic), *The Bridge on the River Kwai* was really one of the first major motion pictures

Col. Nicholson (Alec Guinness) and his Creation, The Bridge on the River Kwai *(Columbia, 1957).*

to open up the entire world of nature to the feature motion picture cameras. In terms of bringing greater realism to their combat fims, this was a major turning point.

David Lean filmed in steaming jungles, amid the constant insect invasion, fighting for the proper atmosphere. His crew which included Oscar winning cameraman Jack Hildyard, waited for the proper sunsets, or the proper skies to add the right touch of nature to the story.

And *The Bridge on the River Kwai* was something else too. It was a "thinking man's spectacle." Like later films such as *Spartacus* and *Lawrence of Arabia*, it avoided the mindlessness of spectacle by offering and emphasizing a superior story that created three dimensional characters. Here, in the jungle, a masterpiece of film engineering was to be created.

Twenty years before Jack Hildyard ever turned a camera, a disillusioned electrical engineering student named Pierre Boulle was contemplating an exodus. He was a bright young student in Paris but he was bored with a tedious existence in secondary school. He yearned for adventure.

If Horace Greely had lived in the City of Light during that spring of 1934, he would have beckoned young Boulle east, not west. In that year, scores of eager young Frenchmen, including some of Boulle's fellow classmates, were leaving France for the East Indian jungles. It was not a quest for gold or oil that was uprooting the youth of France. Nor was it an obsession with diamonds or other precious gems. It was rubber, and a world that now ran on automobile tires was hungry for the stuff.

To the French, the rubber planters were the new pioneers. They were a tough adventuresome breed, men who had carved plantations out of the jungle, organized native labor and established a ready market for one of the world's most promising industries.

Seeking to join them, Boulle left school and headed for the city of Kuala Lampur, the Malayan gateway to the rubber country. He was soon introduced to François de Langlade, a mystery man who would one day become exiled Gen. Charles De Gaulle's clandestine representative in Indochina. During a three year apprenticeship, Boulle learned all about the rubber trade, and he made friends among the other rubber planters, a motley *pot pourri* of former Army officers, office managers and school teachers.

Meanwhile, political events were catching up with the French in Indochina. Following the invasion of China in the fall of 1937, Japanese imperialism proved far more urgent to the planters than the European war which engulfed France two years later. The Japanese Army would soon be pushing into the rubber country, and Boulle realized that there was little to stop them.

When the French Army was demobilized in the late summer of 1941, a Japanese takeover became a foregone conclusion. With no army to protect them, the planters scattered. Boulle fled to Singapore, hoping to make contact with France's last line of defense, the Free French Forces.

At the bar of Singapore's Hotel Adelphi, he found his old boss Langlade and the other planters plotting guerrilla warfare against the advancing Japanese. As he listened, Pierre Boulle began a series of observations that would eventually lead to a novel entitled (in French) *Le Pont de la rivière Kwai*.

In early 1941, only months before their Singapore base was overrun by General Yamashita's Imperial Guard, British Army Intelligence foresaw the importance and desirability of a future guerrilla operation and began secretly training the French irregulars.

Their headquarters at Tanjong-Ralai (about 17 miles from Singapore) was disguised as a convent and it was here that a commando group later known as 136th Army (Kwai's Force 316) was born. In the huge plantation house located at the mouth of a river in the heart of a forest reserve, reconstructed tree for tree like the jungle which would later become his theater of operations, Boulle received instruction in British commando tractics. He learned how to sink a cargo ship in port with the aid of a magnetic cupping glass, how to silently dispose of an enemy sentry, how to blacken the face with any means available, how to derail a train, how to raise a bridge, and even more importantly, how to blow up a train and a bridge.

British colonels Gavin and Chapman found their students avid learners, and it wasn't long before the French planters were ready to put their training to the test. Langlade, who had become their leader, suggested that they quickly organize an expedition to Indochina. Not only would the sortie apply a needed edge to their training, but, as the Japanese were streadily moving south, it would most likely be the last chance to disembark materials for their future sabotage operations.

The basic problem was transportation. Catalina seaplanes, the old inter-island workhorses, were now obsolete. British submarines were unavailable, and the American B-24 Liberator bomber (from which Boulle's future saboteurs were launched for the Kwai) was still a drawing on the table of a Consolidated Aircraft design engineer.

In desperation, the group commandeered a converted houseboat, which had only recently transported passengers along the Shanghai River. They departed Tanjong-Ralai in September

1941. Hugging the Malay peninsula, they headed north, conserving fuel whenever possible in preparation for the dash across the South China Sea.

Fortunately, considering the unseaworthiness of their ancient vessel, a decoded radio message advised them that a major Japanese battle fleet stood in their way. Langlade canceled the operation and they turned around and headed back to Singapore where Pierre Boulle resumed his work as an office clerk.

Three months later, Malaya and the Pacific Islands were invaded by the Japanese. It was soon obvious that the British would not be able to hold out, so it was decided Langlade's Free French should go to China. In January 1942, Pierre Boulle left for Rangoon, Burma. Langlade had intimated that China would be a favorable meeting place for their projected forays into Indochina, so for three weeks Boulle waited for authorization to enter. Finally, he offered his services as a chauffeur, and at the wheel of a Buick destined for the English consul general in Kunming, he drove through Burma. The spirit of adventure present throughout his later novel can be traced back to these chaotic days along the Burmese border.

Reunited once again with Langlade and the planters, Boulle contacted the Chinese military authorities to obtain their support in crossing the Indochinese frontier. While the political and military picture along the border was slowly deteriorating, the Chinese continued their entanglement in ponderous bureaucratic procedures that would eventually handcuff their armies in the field. It was only after interminable feasts with overbearing Chinese authorities that permission to cross the frontier was finally granted.

Once the band crossed the border, however, the situation soon brightened. The supplies secretly acquired by Langlade finally arrived. Arms, radios, boxes of preserves, folding beds, and medications were all in their possession and plans for their first operation were begun.

In June 1942, Boulle and Langlade arrived by mule train in the village of Ba Van which lay in the strategically located Nam Na River Valley, the waterway of which penetrated the Indochinese frontier. On several occasions Boulle journeyed to the frontier to examine the possibilities of crossing. He suggested to the weary

Langlade that they journey to Hanoi by water. He figured that by utilizing the Nam Na River, they could cross into Indochina, branch off to the River Noire, and then ride the current to the Red River which would lead them directly into Hanoi.

To young Boulle, the descent of the rapids from Ba Van to Hanoi, a 450-mile journey, seemed an athletic exercise, which he hoped to accomplish in six nights, resting and hiding by day. Langlade, though, was skeptical. The more so since he could not accompany Boulle on the expedition, being recalled to London by the Free French Committee. After many hesitations, he authorized Boulle to make the journey alone.

Boulle began by constructing a raft, which he reinforced with Chinese string and large bamboos to form a solid, if not comfortable, platform. With a few items of clothes, so as not to arrive in Hanoi too lightly dressed, and an English-Chinese dictionary which could serve for code, all of which was carefully packed in a case of rainproof material, Pierre Boulle was ready for the great adventure.

The most difficult problem was first to find a part of the Nam Na that was even theoretically navigable. The guides who had accompanied him to the frontier had left and Boulle found himself alone in the jungle darkness, on the bank of a stream. After attempting a descent and finding himself in the middle of a rice paddy, he finally discovered a tributary of the Nam Na capable of transporting him through a network of irrigation canals without risk of discovery. For three days and three nights, Boulle braved the jungle on the waterway living the ordeal that the later film, would reserve for commander Shears (William Holden)—the escape from the River Kwai.

Caught by whirlpools which suspended the raft for hours, buffeted brutally in his descent of the rapids, touched with fever, overwhelmed with fatigue, too exhausted even to light a cigarette to burn off the leeches that clung to his legs or to fight against the invasion of ants that were crawling over his body, Boulle continue his push towards Hanoi, still hundreds of miles to the East.

The dawn of the fourth day found him sick with dizziness. He could no longer find concealment. The jungle had given way to rice fields where Thai peasants curiously watched the exhausted white man drift by on the nightmarishly slow-moving river.

Frenchman Pierre Boulle, author of the novel The Bridge on the River Kwai, *as he looked in 1957.*

As his raft approached a forest, Boulle seized the opportunity to land, only to find himself facing thirty angry Thais advancing toward him. His fate was sealed.

Instead of finding himself among friendly villagers, as Shears would in the film, Boulle had beached on military land in the territory of Laichau, about 250 miles northwest of Hanoi. He knew that the peasants had orders to stop all suspects found on such territory. Fearful of being handed over to the Japanese (he was unaware that they were still far to the East), Boulle pretended to be a tourist.

His captors carried him bodily to the nearest village where he was inspected by the Thai militia and locked in a makeshift room. Meanwhile, his raft had been carefully stripped. In a state of exhaustion and fever, Boulle fell asleep. He was later awakened by a French speaking native inspector of the guard who entered the room and questioned him.

Boulle told his interrogator that he was from Ba Van on the other side of the frontier and that some emissaries he had sent to the Indochinese zone had assured him that the commander of the territory of Laichau was sympathetic to the Free French. The inspector listened intently, but said nothing. After twenty minutes, he excused himself and left.

Two days later, Boulle was taken to the French commander of the territory. After weighing the matter carefully, he had decided to reveal his true identity, as well as the reasons which had brought him, like a French Moses, to Laichau.

When brought before the Commander, he declared at once, "I am an officer of the Free French. Can you help me?"

The Commander looked at Boulle, got up slowly and began speaking in a confident manner. "I wish for the Allied victory, but the Gaullists are misled and acting against the best interests of France. I shall always remain faithful to the Marshal [Pétain] who wants to maintain discipline at all costs. Discipline is essential at this moment above everything moral. I cannot help you. It is thus necessary for me to arrest you."

In this incredibly stubborn Frenchman, Boulle had found the prototype for his main character in *The Bridge on the River Kwai*, the English colonel, Nicholson. During a two-year prison sentence, Boulle began fashioning the notes that would eventually lead to his novel.

American screenwriter Carl Foreman was exiled in London when Boulle's original French novel was published in 1952. Foreman's troubles had begun the previous fall. In a prepared statement read before the House Committee on Un-American Activities (then investigating reports of Communist subversion in the motion picture industry), Foreman admitted a one-time association with the Communist Party, but assured the Commmittee that he had terminated all ties in 1949. His admission proved unsatisfactory. When asked to reveal names, Foreman refused, pleading the Fifth Amendment.

Producer Stanley Kramer immediately severed their partnership, and Foreman's name began to appear on the Committee's "uncooperative list." Blacklisting in Hollywood soon followed.

Unable to find work in California or New York, despite the support of staunch anticommunists such as actor Gary Cooper, Foreman went to London, a bitter and disillusioned writer. In the spring of 1952, he was confronted by State Department officials who pulled his passport.

Fortunately for Foreman, English producer Alexander Korda had respect for his talents and ignoring the blacklist situation in America, signed Foreman on as a producer/writer with Korda's own production company, London Films.

Foreman was struggling through Pierre Boulle's French prose when Major Ian Fielding's English translation of *The Bridge on the River Kwai* first appeared. It was one book that begged for dramatization.

"The thing that struck me about the book," he recalls, "entirely apart from the fact that it technically was an English subject and could be a British film (and I had to make British films at that time because of the blacklist), was the fact that a Frenchman was taking a hard, objective, and yet cynical, look at both the British and Japanese military officer castes.

"What Boulle was saying in terms of his two leading characters, Colonel Nicholson, and Colonel Saito, the commandant of the Japanese prison camp, was that they were very much alike. If anything, they were two sides of the same coin. He was making other statements as well, perhaps having fun with the notion that the English and Japanese were also similiar because they were both island people."

Although French producer Henri Georges Cluzot of *Les Diaboliques* fame had optioned screen rights immediately after Boulle's novel was published, he had been unable to raise enough money to begin production. Foreman purchased Cluzot's option for a paltry $850 (10 per cent of the total purchase price, on a six month option). The following day, Foreman presented the project

Producer Sam Spiegel, Sessue Hayakawa and Alec Guinness shoot the breeze between takes at Mahara, Ceylon. — The Bridge on the River Kwai *(Columbia, 1957).*

to Korda as his first venture under the Union Jack. Korda was uninterested.

"In fact," says Foreman, "he hated the book. He failed to understand the character of Colonel Nicholson. He saw him as a madman. Holding that viewpoint, he felt that the English public could never accept such a character."

Foreman did not want to give up the novel, but he couldn't bankroll the film himself either. He would have to search for another producer to put up the funds. Two days after Korda thumbed-down the project, Foreman heard from American producer Sam Spiegel who was also in love with the Boulle novel.

Spiegel had just completed *On the Waterfront*, a film which was soon to sweep the 1954 Academy Awards. Interestingly, it was one of the few films Spiegel had ever filmed within the borders of the United States.

Like Pierre Boulle, Sam Spiegel was an adventurer at heart. Born in Jareslau, Austria, on November 11, 1902, he had spent much of his youth as a "young pioneer" in Palestine. In 1928, he arrived in Hollywood where he began working as a production assistant at Universal Pictures. In 1930 production chief Carl Laemmle sent him to Europe to handle overseas production. It was a powerful position for the young adventurer and in his dealings with foreign governments, especially during the political chicanery associated with the marketing of Universal's *All Quiet on the Western Front* in Europe, Spiegel was introduced to such notables as Adolf Hitler, Joseph Goebbels and Benito Mussolini. But Spiegel was Jewish and time was running out for the Jews in Europe. When Hitler rose to power in 1933, Spiegel fled to Hollywood.

After World War II he formed Horizon Pictues with director John Huston. The pair's greatest success was *The African Queen* (1951), with a screenplay by James Agee, which won for Humphrey Bogart his only Academy Award.

Following *On the Waterfront*, Spiegel left for Europe. In July 1954 he met director Elia Kazan in Paris, where they discussed a possible film version of Paul Osborne's 1939 play, *Morning's at Seven*. While in Paris, he became enchanted with *The Bridge on the River Kwai*, then available in translation.

Through French producer Henri Cluzot, he learned that

"You and that Colonel Nicholson are just alike!" bellows Major Shears (William Holden) to a wounded Major Warden. — The Bridge on the River Kwai *(Columbia, 1957).*

Foreman had already purchased an option on the screen rights, and later the same day he was told that Alexander Korda had promptly rejected the project. Spiegel contacted Foreman and at a secret meeting place in England (Foreman could not journey to Paris because of his restricted passport) bought the screen rights for $7000. Foreman also agreed to write the screenplay for an additional $10,000.

That an American producer had purchased Boulle's novel proved quite significant in terms of the projected film. One of Spiegel's first directives to Foreman, was to create an American character in the story for boxoffice purposes.

Major Shears, the English commando in the novel, was changed to Commander Shears, the American opportunist in the film. Foreman still retained the overriding conflict between Nicholson and Saito, along with the important themes on madness and hypocrisy in the Siamese jungle of 1943. Foreman was also fascinated by Boulle's use of irony throughout the novel. "After all," says Foreman, "the whole thrust of Boulle's novel was that whatever man planned or tried or essayed, he was always subject to natural law which in a sense made him small and powerless. This was to be a recurring theme throughout the entire film."

In the late winter of 1954-55, after signing British actors Jack Hawkins and Charles Laughton to play Warden and Nicholson respectively, and David Lean as director and Jack Hildyard as cinematographer, Sam Spiegel began the first of four trips around the world in search of locations. Columbia Pictures had agreed to finance the motion picture; the question remained, where to film?

Hoping to find the actual bridge site, Spiegel, Lean and Hildyard embarked for the jungles of Siam, which turned out to be a major disappointment. Not only were there no roads to carry in or maneuver a cast of several hundred actors and a sizeable crew, but the River Kwai, which actually runs there, proved from a purely cinematic point of view, to be quite small and uninteresting.

When Spiegel mentioned his observations to his guide, he was informed that the Malay Peninsula was unmatched in scenic beauty. The scouting unit moved south to the river country only to see their potential locations overrun with communist guerrillas.

Two armored trucks were assigned to protect them, but when one of the vehicles was captured and half of its occupants killed, Spiegel decided to abandon the reconnaissance. Exhausted after a month's travel, Lean suggested that they recuperate at Mount Lavinia, a seaside resort on the island of Ceylon.

Ceylon is a magical island whose history is steeped in legend. According to one Islamic tale, it was to Ceylon that Adam and Eve fled once life became too harsh in the Garden of Eden. With its varied landscape, Spiegel quickly realized that Ceylon was ideally suited to Boulle's wideranging novel.

Although not the first producer to stumble upon the island's native charm (between 1952 and 1955, the island had been used as a location in such films as *Outpost in Malaya, Elephant Walk, The Beachcomber,* and *The Purple Plain*), Spiegel's crew would be the first to record its beauty with a Cinemascope camera. With the location set, Spiegel returned to Hollywood to organize a major crew and to continue casting, leaving Lean and Hildyard in Colombo, the island's capital, to search out the exact location for the bridge and the prison camp. They were soon joined by art director Donald Ashton, his assistant Geoffrey Drake and Carl Foreman, who delivered to Lean a completed first draft screenplay.

Ashton was a particularly valuable asset. Stationed in Ceylon with the British Army during the Second World War, he had married a planter's daughter at war's end. With his keen knowledge of the countryside, the crew had little trouble finding locales to match the actual sites depicted in Boulle's novel.

In an abandoned stone quarry in Mahara, Ashton planted the Japanese Imperial Army pennant and began construction on Colonel Saito's prison camp, No. 16. It would take five months to complete. In the absence of dump trucks and steam shovels, elephants were the prime movers during the construction phase. On film, the finished camp is a nest of scraggly bamboo huts beset by swarms of mosquitoes and surrounded by hundreds of makeshift wooden crosses marking the graves of Camp 16's former tenants.

It was the construction of the bridge, though, that symbolized Spiegel's supreme quest for ultimate authenticity. Based upon a sketch of an actual railroad bridge scribbled on a tattered

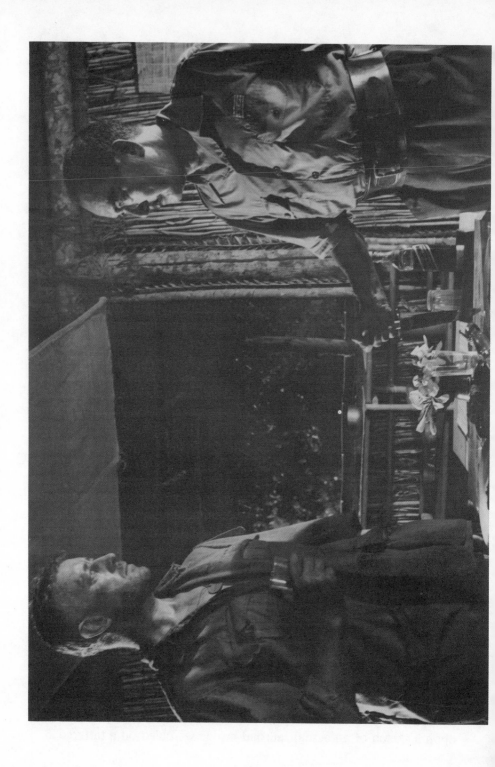

piece of cigarette paper and smuggled across the Burma-Siam border into Lord Louis Mountbatten's Southeast Asia Headquarters in Ceylon, the Kwai bridge became the largest outdoor set in history.

A third longer than a football gridiron and as tall as a six story building, it would take six months to build with Ceylonese labor and elephants, at a total cost of $250,000. With the original sketch in hand, Spiegel hired a London based engineering film to draw up the actual plans for the bridge.

Ashton surveyed several Ceylonese rivers before he spotted the proper location across the Kilaniya River at Kitulgala, 56 miles northeast of Colombo.

Reinforced by 48 elephants, numbered for easy identification like so many football fullbacks, several hundred workers began work on the bridge in the early spring of 1956. Fifteen hundred trees were cut down in the surrounding forest and fashioned into pillars, which were transported by elephants across manmade roads and a specially constructed trestle bridge to Kitulgala where they were piledriven into the ground to create a structure larger than any in Ceylon (425 feet long and 90 feet high).

As work progressed on the bridge throughout the summer and early fall of 1956. Spiegel resumed his international search for his cast. In August he went to Tokyo and signed Sessue Hayakawa, a former American silent film star, for the important role of Colonel Saito, the prison camp commandant.

Back in Colombo, Carl Foreman was encountering increasing difficulties in fashioning the final shooting script. Between Boulle's cynicism, Spiegel's commercialism, and Lean's stubborn Britishness (he was also a stickler for detail), Foreman's patience was wearing very thin.

The primary sore point concerned the film's ending. In the novel, Nicholson discovers Force 316's demolition cables, betrays the sabotage to the Japanese and dies in a hail of shrapnel from Warden's mortar bombs. The bridge remains standing, and Force

---

Facing page: *A confrontation of immovables: Col. Saito (Sessue Hayakawa, right) threatens Col. Nicholson (Alec Guinness) with punishment unless his officers work on* The Bridge on the River Kwai *(Columbia, 1957).*

316's mission is a failure. Spiegel rejected Boulle's ending. He saw the blowing of the bridge as a potentially awesome cinematic event, rivaling Cecil B. DeMille's parting of the Red Sea in his just released *The Ten Commandments*. Accordingly, he ordered Foreman to rewrite Boulle's finale, having the British commandos succeed in blowing the bridge just as a ceremonial Japanese train, loaded with dignitaries, enters the gorge.

David Lean was concerned with the question of whether or not Colonel Nicholson, by leading the Japanese, in the novel, to the demolition cables, was involved in the act of treason. Was it treason or insanity?

Says Foreman, "Being British, David was quite sensitive about the impression Nicholson would give to an audience. In my opinion, it was never treason. But it was the ultimate insanity. This man had built a bridge and the bridge had become more important to him than the entire war."

Lean agreed with Foreman, "in most movies about war, people are conceived and conceived of as heroes. Aren't they wonderful. There was no question that Nicholson was a very brave man, but wasn't he also a fool who in the end became a blithering idiot?"

Although writer and director agreed upon Nicholson's basic motivation, a conflict revolved around the manner of his death and the fate of the bridge. Did Nicholson actually fall on the detonator purposefully in the film, after being hit by Warden's mortar bombs? Or was it entirely an accident that he fell on the plunger just as the train hit the bridge?

"In my ending," says Foreman, "the bridge was blown up, but again, by the same stroke of ironic chance that pervaded the whole film, it was only partially destroyed, and remained standing. The Colonel did not throw his body on the detonator. David and I discussed this scene many times and I thought this would be wrong. David always wanted Nicholson to do something that would expiate his previous actions, the discovery of the cables, the death of Lieutenant Joyce, the death of Shears et al. I disagreed because any last minute reformation would have been a serious copout."

Whether Lean's sense of ultimate honor and justice or Foreman's quest for irony prevailed was not the ultimate question.

It was still Spiegel's show and in his own mind, the destiny of the film's finale lay in spectacle, not irony.

A frustrated Foreman bided his time, attempting to reconcile his differences with Lean. It was another development, however, that eventually forced the point. In the early summer of 1956, Foreman had written to the House Committee on Un-American Activities requesting another interview. In a June 1961 interview, he recalled the anxieties of his original appearance: "My mistake was in standing on the Fifth Amendment instead of the First. The First Amendment guarantees freedom of speech; the Fifth, against 'self incrimination,' implies you've got something to hide, something you feel guilty of, or ashamed of, something criminal. I had nothing to hide. But, at the time, I was ill advised."

Granted a new interview, Foreman stood before the Committee that August, and after being termed a fine patriotic American, was given a clean bill of health. For the first time in five years, he could return to work in the United States. Rumors were rife that Columbia was offering him a multi-picture production contract. Foreman was no longer the black-listed exile; he had unstuck himself.

It was certainly a good excuse to wave goodbye to Lean. Outnumbered and having lost his last measure of creative control on the project, Foreman left Ceylon and asked Spiegel for his release. Spiegel was sympathetic and asked Foreman to recommend another writer who could work with Lean.

Foreman recommended Michael Wilson, another Hollywood blacklisted exile, then living in Paris. He explained to Spiegel that Wilson would be quite willing to work anonymously for a reasonable sum. Spiegel thanked Foreman, took down Wilson's name and address and hired, instead, Calder Willingham, who spent three horrid weeks in Colombo, got fed up with Lean and departed.

Foreman points out that Lean wanted a British writer if one could be found. "Underneath it all, this was our major problem. We were divided by a common language!"

Eventually, Spiegel took Foreman's advice and persuaded Lean to try Wilson. At last the collaboration succeeded. Wilson, who had previously worked with William Wyler on *Friendly Persuasion*, arrived from Paris, checked into Colombo's Galle-Face

Hotel and began rewriting Foreman's first draft screenplay. The first ten days were spent in conference with Lean and Spiegel where agreement was finally reached on the general thrust of his rewriting. It was pointed out that aside from reworking the ending, his primary task was now to develop a new character for Commander Shears, the American, and to make his role equal in stature to that of the British and Japanese colonels. He was to do the same for the role of Warden, the British commando officer.

For nine weeks, throughout August and September of 1956, Wilson, working closely with Lean, rewrote and completed the final script of *The Bridge on the River Kwai*. At his insistence, there were no daily conferences, and meetings with Lean occurred only when he had completed a long sequence of 20 to 30 pages.

Remembers Wilson, "My relationship with David Lean was a good one, although he was not an easy man to please. Meticulous in all respects, he did not readily commit himself to some of my new ideas, although in time he came to accept most of them."

One of Wilson's primary contributions was the controversial, albeit secondary, conflict formulated between Shears and Warden. In following Boulle's novel, Foreman had justifiably given the pair subordinate roles. In building up their parts on Spiegel's orders, Wilson introduced certain salient features to Warden's makeup that made him appear similiar in character to Colonel Nicholson, a factor that created natural conflict with the opportunistic American, Shears.

When Spiegel signed actor William Holden to play Shears, Wilson was able to rework certain elements of the popular Sefton part that won Holden an Oscar for *Stalag 17* three years earlier. Shears, like Sefton, a prisoner in a German prison camp, became an opportunist intent on surviving the war at all costs.

In late September 1956, Charles Laughton, Spiegel's original choice for Nicholson, asked for his release so that he could rejoin the Broadway production of *Major Barbara*. The producer's only other choice for the part was Alec Guinness, who, unfortunately, had already refused the part several times. Guin-

---

Facing page: *An enraged Lt. Joyce (Geoffrey Horne, right) turns on Col. Saito (Hayakawa, center), ignoring his true enemy, Col. Nicholson (Guinness).* — The Bridge on the River Kwai *(Columbia, 1957).*

ness claimed that his fans knew him primarily as a comedian and moviegoers, he concluded, could never accept him as the rabidly austere, honorable Lt. Col. Nicholson.

But Spiegel wanted him. Accompanied by Lean, who had directed Guinness before in such films as *Great Expectations* (1947) and *Oliver Twist* (1948), he flew to London for one final effort and visited the actor who was then working on the stage production of *Hotel Paradiso*.

Spiegel invited him to dinner after a midweek performance. The actor reiterated that it was useless, but nonetheless accepted the dinner invitation graciously. It is a credit to Spiegel that by dessert time, Guinness had accepted the part.

While in London, Spiegel also signed actor James Donald to play Clifton, the dry, witty, medical officer whose final cry of "Madness! Madness!" when the bridge is blown and everyone lies dead, ends the film.

From London, Spiegel winged west to Hollywood, leaving copies of the completed script with Cary Grant and William Holden. Before Grant could even glance at the script, Holden (then Hollywood's No. 1 boxoffice attraction) had read it, become enchanted with the Shears part, phoned Spiegel accepting the role, and made preparations for his departure that winter.

Holden's new contract, signed one week after his arrival in Colombo, was a financial milestone. He would receive a basic salary of $250,000, plus 10 per cent of the film's gross receipts in excess of $2.5 million. For his work on *The Bridge on the River Kwai*, Holden would eventually see over $2 million. Spiegel's cast now included two of the world's top stars. Jack Hawkins, previously signed for the part of Warden was, then, England's No. 1 boxoffice attraction.

After a brief trip to Ceylon to witness the commencement of preproduction second unit photography, Spiegel began a concentrated search for a youthful actor to play Lieutenant Joyce, as well as several actresses to add still more commercial value to the film. Holden without a love interest was commercially unthinkable.

The search for Joyce, the young commando officer whose indecisiveness jeopardizes the entire mission, took a great deal of time. After a hundred unrewarding interviews, Spiegel paused in his search to attend the New York premiere of his production *The Strange One*, which Horizon Pictures had filmed in Florida. In the small part of a military college cadet who is brutally beaten, Spiegel spotted young Geoffrey Horne and was immediately captivated by his sensitive performance. In a movie he had produced himself, Spiegel had discovered his green commando.

With principle photography due to begin in less than a month, Spiegel quickly signed lovely Anne Sears to play opposite Holden in the Ceylon love scenes (later filmed at Mount Lavinia where a beach resort was hastily converted into a British Army Hospital).

November 1956 dawned auspiciously. The bridge was completed, hundreds of extras were signed, and David Lean was ready to begin work with the actors. Filming began in the prison camp at Mahara on the 26th. Every day the location company hired a special train to carry the hundreds of extras needed for the prison camp scenes. Dubbed the "Spiegel Special," it left Colombo every morning at 4:00 a.m. Shooting didn't begin until 9:00 a.m. but the task of making up the huge number of extras to look like halfstarved prisoners took nearly four hours.

In keeping with the film's ever-present irony, most of the Japanese soldiers portrayed as camp guards were actually Chinese. Several of the British prisoners were Italians and Germans, many of the sunburnt Australians were fair-skinned Asiatics, and all of the Indians were Ceylonese.

After a spirited New Years Eve celebration, Lean shifted his cameras to the Kitulgala Valley location, site of Ceylon's newest tourist attraction, "The Bridge," He would return to Mahara briefly for a set of exteriors with newly arrived William Holden. The latter's arrival in Colombo on December 8th, rivaled the welcome given Queen Elizabeth earlier in the year. Exotic dancers from Kandy piped him from his plane to customs while Ceylon's prettiest maidens threw perfumed flowers at his feet and a baby elephant carried his bag.

Surrounded by the lush Ceylonese landscape and given his characteristic desire for perfection, David Lean seldom missed a chance to blend superb acting with symbolic atmosphere. Throughout the film, Lean used the colorful jungle backgrounds as integral parts of the film's action sequences. He often painted

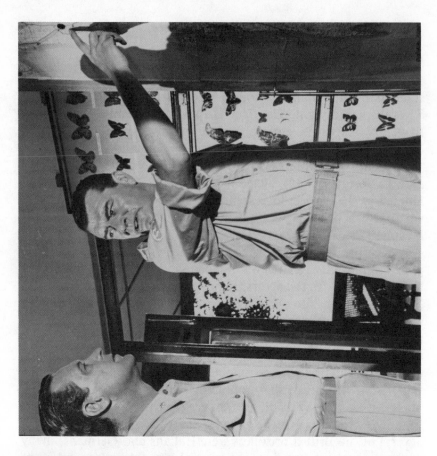

the jungle in several moods. Quiet and mysterious when Joyce and Warden track the lone Japanese soldier, it becomes cruel and unyielding during the final trek to the bridge. Composer Malcolm Arnold would later give these latter scenes a grandly adventuresome quality in a musical score that won the Oscar that year.

Lean portrays the River Kwai as being rich and vibrant with activity at night when Joyce and Shears place the explosive charges, but this changes in the morning when the river becomes quiet and foreboding, its exposed banks and wallows symbolic of a hidden truth.

Lean's powerful visual sense and Alec Guinness' new found enthusiasm for the character of Colonel Nicholson eventually collided, one night, in early February 1957. In a poignant night sequence, Nicholson and Saito meet on the just completed bridge. Nicholson quietly discusses his life in the military, while his captor looks on silently. At a precise moment, while he was leaning against one of the bridge's hand rails, the script called for Nicholson to drop his officer's baton into the river. The camera follows the baton down where it falls next to a blackfaced Shears who is placing the explosives that will destroy the bridge.

Lean planned to shoot the sequence just prior to sunset, a time that symbolized the destiny of two highly similiar soldiers. Jack Hildyard waited for just the right moment, when the sun was just visible through the trees. When all was perfect, Lean gave the order to "roll-em," and Guinness was given his cue. Unfortunately, he failed to drop his baton.

"My dear fellow," he explained to the exasperated director, "it's simply not in character. No British officer would ever drop his baton."

Lean replied, "But Alec, that's what I want!"

Guinness apologized, "I'm sorry, but at that moment I was so into the character that I couldn't do it."

"All right," said Lean, "let's come back tomorrow and do it again." He dismissed the crew and retired to Colombo.

Facing page, left: *Anne Sears portraying the obligatory romantic figure for William Holden's Major Shears.* Right: *"You were picked up here," Major Warden (Jack Hawkins) tells Shears*—The Bridge on the River Kwai *(Columbia, 1957).*

The next evening the crews were once more in position, waiting for the appropriate moment. The same thing occurred.

"My God, Alec!" Lean roared, "come on now, what are you doing?"

"I'm sorry David, I just faced that moment, and I couldn't do it. I was in the military you know, and *you just wouldn't drop your baton*!"

"But Alec, we have to finish this scene, and if you don't drop that baton...."

Fortunately for the picture's budget and Lean's patience, Alec Guinness did drop the baton on the third night. His only comment: "Well, I did it, but I don't think it's right."

With the bridge exteriors completed, Alec Guinness returned to London. Preparations were now made to blow up the $250,000 set.

Spiegel had been planning the demolition for two years. Several cameras would record the tremendous blast, the collapse of the bridge, and the fall into the gorge of an overaged train which had been purchased from the Ceylonese government. It was obviously the film's single most delicate scene. If the train was blown off the bridge prematurely, there was no chance for a second take.

For the sabotage sequence, the producer imported a select team from Imperial Chemical in London. The demolitions experts, skilled in using large quantities of explosives, studied every plank of the bridge for weeks. While the film's Force 316 utilizes a relatively modest amount of plastic explosive in their handiwork, the men from Imperial surmised that it would take at least a thousand pounds of Glasgow dynamite to blow the train off the bridge.

"Even then," said one expert, "nobody knows whether the bridge will blow up or merely be knocked down. This is because the bridge is so heavy and so high. Also, if the explosives are placed underneath the log supports, the supports could break like matchsticks under the weight above, forcing the bridge to tip over into the river rather than lifting the bridge and train in the grand style which audiences accustomed to watching Hollywood's miniature explosions expect."

As a necessary precaution, Spiegel asked for and was given

The bridge is blown and Producer Spiegel gets his spectacular ending. — The Bridge on the River Kwai *(Columbia, 1957).*

a detachment of soldiers to guard the bridge against premature sabotage. The night after the demolition charges had been carefully placed, a truck carrying gasoline mysteriously caught fire, a few yards from the bridge. The driver jumped from the blazing vehicle which headed out of control towards the bridge. Quick as lightning, the Ceylonese soldiers risked their lives to head the truck off and turn it down a steep precipice. It finally landed in the river where it exploded at a safe distance from the bridge.

Finally, on the morning of March 11, 1957, everything was ready. Four cameras, safely dug into sandbagged emplacements, were in position to record the explosion at close range. Slightly out of range, members of the cast and crew waited expectantly in another series of bunkers, their own cameras trained on the doomed bridge. Hovering overhead, an RAF helicopter contained a fifth camera ready to shoot the explosion from still another angle.

For the ground emplacements, it was arranged by Lean that the cameramen would all leave their cameras a few moments before the explosion and proceed to places of safety. All the ground units had been wired so that the cameramen could press a button which would inform producer Spiegel, in a command bunker, that they were safe and that their cameras were in working order. Spiegel would then give the signal to the men from Imperial to blow the bridge.

A human error nearly cost Spiegel all the months of effort and expense. In his excitement, one cameraman forgot to press his safety button. As the, now unstoppable, train rolled forward, thoughts raced through the producer's mind. This was the moment of the biggest scene in the film, but if one cameramen had not reached his place of safety, he might still be hurt, even killed.

Spiegel ordered the demoliton halted. The 65-year-old locomotive rode across the bridge unharmed, over the few feet of rail extending beyond and ploughed off the track (ironically, in Pierre Boulle's novel, the Japanese train actually makes it across the bridge only to be blown over by a lone charge placed by a second-guessing Warden).

After this near disaster, the elephants were ordered forward and the repair work began. Throughout the day and night of March 11th, the crew repaired the damage, lifted the train back onto the track and once more backed it to its starting point.

At two minutes before ten on the morning of March 12th, the green lights began to flash in Spiegel's command bunker. Loud speakers blared forth a final warning to the few spectators within the danger area. Actors William Holden, Jack Hawkins, and Geoffrey Horne retreated to their sand-bagged emplacements. A few trucks sped off down the Kitulgala-Colombo road.

Hundreds of cameras and binoculars focused on the bridge. Lean's tape recorders awoke to the sound of a train whistle. A thin puff of smoke signaled the approach of the doomed locomotive. Awakened from their sleep, a few jungle birds flew skyward.

At exactly ten o'clock, Spiegel gave the signal to Imperial Chemical. A thousand pounds of dynamite ignited by a maze of circuitry ripped the bridge apart. As the bridge collapsed, the overage locomotive arrived to fall expertly into the gorge along with its passenger cars. It was a spectacular sequence, well worth the effort and suspense.

Locomotive steam was still rising above the Kitulgala Valley when a motorcycle escort convoyed the precious film cargo to Colombo Airport. Spiegel was taking no chances. Five different airplanes would transport the explosion footage to processing labs in London.

Minutes after the explosion, souvenir hunters, ignoring the repeated warnings, swarmed over the bridge's fallen timbers. Others took undamaged timber for practical purposes, like building fences and sheds. Parts of the train were gathered by junk men for scrap metal. Its manmade dam eliminated, the torrential Kilaniva River later swept away most of what remained.

7

A Difference in Style

Fully one year before he began his Oscar-winning screen-play for the 1949 film, *Battleground*, screenwriter Robert Pirosh accidentally stumbled across the details to one of World War II's most bizarre incidents, a multi-unit deception that would lead the Americans to victory in the Battle of the Bulge, and Pirosh to one of the best combat films of the Sixties: *Hell Is for Heroes.*

In the spring of 1946, Pirosh was enroute to his new writing assignment at the Samuel Goldwyn Studios, in Hollywood, when he stopped in a gas station for a fillup. New clothing was still scarce in postwar California, so the combat veteran was making good use out of his military uniform, which included the "ruptured duck" insignia of all dischargees. Noticing the emblem, the service station attendant, himself a veteran, struck up a conversation, during which Pirosh revealed that he was a veteran of the 35th Infantry Division.

"35th Division!" cried the attendant, "I'll never forget that outfit. When they pulled you guys out of the Vosges Mountains and sent you to the Bulge, they sent in my unit to cover your positions. It was a secret move, a deception, and we were small. Our job was to spread out very thin and hold, hoping that the Germans wouldn't discover the switch."

At the moment, Pirosh did not know that he was listening to a military secret. Or that the deception pulled in the Ardennes that winter of 1944, a secret maneuver allowing the Allied High Command to quickly shift the axis of an entire Allied Army and deploy it against the German counteroffensive, would remain classified until 1960. Pirosh recorded the details of the maneuver in his diary, thanked the attendant, and reported to work. For nine years, the story remained buried in his notebook.

In the summer of 1955, after completing *Girl Rush*, a minor musical starring Rosalind Russell, he began searching for a new project. While thumbing through his wartime diary, he discovered the few scribbles he had once haphazardly recorded.

A new war film project seemed appealing to him. He had enjoyed the success of *Battleground*, and *Go for Broke*, the latter a combat film depicting the story of the 442nd Regimental Combat Team, the Japanese-American unit that had distinguished itself in Italy.

Pirosh put through a call to an established contact in Washington, but the response was unsettling. The "Vosges Deception" was still classified. He was pondering his next move when the telephone rang. It was Ray Stark, a major theatrical agent (later a famous producer) with an offer. The Kirk Douglas Company was producing a film version of the popular television show, *Spring Reunion*. A director was needed and Pirosh had been highly recommended.

Just the thought of a long research trip to Washington with the possibility of major haggling with the Pentagon made him opt for the new project. The war film could wait. There was, after all, no danger of anyone's stealing his idea—Army red tape would see to that.

Spring Reunion, which featured Betty Hutton, Dana Andrews and Jean Hagen, was released in late 1957. Filmed at a rented studio and allowed a cramped budget, it turned out to be less than the interesting project Pirosh had envisioned. Three years went by. The writer-director began developing an idea for a television series based on his wartime diary. *Combat*, the product of his labors, debuted in the fall of 1962. It remains today the most successful military drama ever shown on national television.

On October 5, 1960, good news arrived from Washington. The 1944 deception had been reclassified and was no longer considered a top military secret. Would Pirosh like the details? Delighted, he dusted off his original five-page treatment, filled in the gaps with historical details and went to visit his friend, Martin Rackin, head of production at Paramount Studios.

Rackin, a relative newcomer at Paramount (he was in the middle of his second year there), was himself a combat veteran, having served as a bomber pilot with General George C. Kenney's

5th Air Force in the Philippines. A few years after the war he had written *Fighter Squadron* (1948), a World War II air saga notable as Rock Hudson's first film.

In what he later referred to as a "real razzle dazzle," Pirosh gave Rackin a rough insight into the 1944 deception: "Marty, it's an amazing story. A ten-man squad is ordered to defend a company's position on the Siegfried Line. I've worked out about five pages to give you an idea as to what kind of gimmicks the men use to trick the enemy."

The gimmicks were unusual and helped to sell the story to Rackin. In the short treatment, Pirosh had his squad modify the engine on an ordinary jeep to make it sound either like a tank or a truck. When driven back and forth behind their positions, it would give the Germans the impression that they were opposed by a company with armored support. Pirosh also had the men string wires in front of their positions. To these they attached empty ammunition cans filled with rocks. The cans were placed at strategic points, so that when they were tripped, it appeared that patrols were out.

Rackin was impressed. Aware of Pirosh's background and professionalism in combat films, coupled with an excellent track record at MGM, he signed the writer to write, produce and direct the proposed film. For the first time in his life, Pirosh would wear all three hats.

Before he left, Rackin asked, "Do you have a title, something I can send to the New York office?

"I thought we would call it "Separation Hill," Pirosh replied, "It's a term we used in the Army when you're on your first big hike and you're going up a steep hill. As trainees begin to drop out, the Sergeant starts yelling, 'Come on men, this is separation hill. It'll separate the men from the boys.'"

With a fat contract under his belt, Pirosh resumed a personal interest in the life of the combat infantryman begun so successfully with *Battleground*. He retained the squad as his basic

---

Facing page: *In a tavern behind the lines, Sergeant Pike (Fess Parker, right) confronts Reese (Steve McQueen) with the news that the company is moving back on the line, in the opening of* Hell Is for Heroes *(Paramount, 1962).*

unit, developing a group of soldiers with certain individual characteristics. In the new film there were men like Sergeant Pike, the tough experienced platoon sergeant; Larkin, the nervous but courageous squad leader; Corby, the hard-bitten scrounger; Henshaw, the fixer, whose only friend was a duck; and Homer, the Polish refugee, one of the story's most unique characters.

The idea of Homer (later portrayed by Nick Adams) came from a true incident depicted in the wartime diary. During the last months of the war, after the 35th Division had crossed the Rhine River and was moving through Germany, Pirosh's squad was assigned the task of reconnoitering evacuated villages. Conversant in German, the Master Sergeant with the makeshift diary in his pack was frequently ordered to take five men and investigate tiny enclaves on the road to Berlin.

During one of these patrols, his unit discovered two German soldiers cowering in a cellar. After a few choice words, they surrendered. "No excitement," as he later recorded. Aside from these ragged remnants of the once proud Wehrmacht, there was another resident of the filthy cellar, a wide-eyed Polish youngster, barely 17 years old, and a recent escapee from a slave labor camp. In German, the boy communicated his sole desire: he wanted to become an American soldier.

Pirosh took the boy back with him and for the next month tried, through every channel, to get him inducted. In the meantime, he became the unit's mascot, learning American mannerisms, and mastering those peculiar American cuss words ever-present in the military ranks. The perpetually cussing youngster, whose name the unit could never pronounce, was christened Homer.

Says Pirosh, "Homer was given a uniform, but we never gave him a rifle. The Army wouldn't let him have one, and rightfully so, for he could have shot one of our own men by mistake."

Eventually, Pirosh regretted his decision to adopt Homer into the unit's ranks. He would get drunk, and though he was a good natured and fun loving kid, he was also very immature and he frequently embarrassed the squad behind the lines. Somehow, he managed to ingratiate himself into another platoon, and the last Pirosh saw of him, he was still in uniform.

The script was half finished when Pirosh began to encounter "writer's block." The characters were intriguing, at times highly amusing. The plot was interesting enough, the deception downright ingenious. But something was lacking, a certain driving force. There was little motivation to all the characters. They were fast becoming just another platoon of guys. The unorthodox deception was in danger of becoming routine.

"I couldn't get off the ground," he recalls. "There I had this big contract, the biggest I had ever had by far, and I couldn't write the complete story. I was stuck, and I floundered for weeks."

The experienced screenwriter he was, Pirosh had a plan of action covering any emergency. This time he went to his former writing partner, George Seaton, for advice. The pair had a useful arrangement, dating back to the 1930's, by which script problems were solved in conference. After reading the "Separation Hill" story, Seaton said that he enjoyed the suspense of the story, but agreed that it lacked the crucial internal conflict. He suggested that Pirosh take one of the characters and turn him into a more interesting person, someone, in fact, a little off center.

"Why don't you make this guy Reese a real psychotic? Seaton advised. "He's a nut and he likes combat. He's also a bastard and the squad stays away from him. But at the same time they respect him because he's a good soldier."

Seaton felt that with a central conflict between Reese and the men, especially Sergeant Larkin who's a book soldier, Pirosh would be able to divide the focus of the screenplay between the deception and Reese.

Pirosh was pleased with the suggestion and began to modify the Reese character. Originally, just an eager beaver GI with a liking for combat, he became a man obsessed. He cannot adjust to life behind the lines. Once, after winning a battlefield commission, Reese went on furlough and cracked up, nearly killing a superior officer in the process. In the Pirosh script, he comes to Pike's squad once more a private. He's a loner, waiting for the next move. He does not identify with his fellow squad members, who are thinking of the war's end and a return to their homes. Reese wants to fight.

To play this character, Rackin signed Steve McQueen, the youthful hero of the *Wanted Dead or Alive* television series and a

recent success in John Sturges' *The Magnificent Seven*. Pirosh also called Rackin's attention to another star of *The Magnificent Seven*, James Coburn. Coburn was signed to play Henshaw, the fixer. Another television personality, Nick Adams of *The Rebel*, was hired to play the Homer character.

Says Pirosh, "I tried very hard to get a real Polish kid to play the part. I figured we could make an actor out of him, like we did in *Go for Broke* with the Nisei. But I just couldn't find anybody that was right for the role. Rackin, who was very good at casting, suggested Nick Adams. I liked Nick and he was a talented guy, but I still think he was too old for the part."

Television's Davy Crockett, Fess Parker, was signed to play Sergeant Pike, the stalwart platoon leader, singer Bobby Darin became the perfect Corby, a guy constantly on the take, and character actor Harry Guardino who had shined in *Pork Chop Hill* in a brief role, became Sergeant Larkin, Reese's major nemesis.

One of the more unusual parts in the film was added at the last moment. This was Private Driscoll, the naive headquarters clerk, a bumbling typist who is "drafted" by Larkin's hardpressed combat squad. He would be played by newcomer Bob Newhart.

Having met the young recording artist at Charlie Morrison's Mocambo Club, Rackin asked Pirosh whether there was some way they could get Newhart into the picture. Together, the two men conceived of the Driscoll character, whose particular talent further aids the deception on the Siegfried Line.

Director Don Siegel, who later replaced Pirosh as the film's director, criticized the way in which Newhart's talent for monologue was exploited: "Bob Newhart could have been accepted if I didn't have to put him through that ridiculous telephone conversation (in the film, Larkin asks Driscoll to imitate a real phone conversation with headquarters for the benefit of German listeners who've wired the unit's command post).

"He could have been amusing and scared and all that, but I

Facing page, top and bottom: *Much of the plot of* Hell Is for Heroes *(Paramount, 1962) revolves around a confrontation between hot shot loner Reese (Steve McQueen, top) and by-the-book soldier Larkin (Harry Guardino).*

wouldn't have him going through his 'shtick' routine. It had no place in the film. I wouldn't even have Bobby Darin singing, something I know the studio would have loved."

In the shadow of Mount Shasta, outside Redding in Northern California, Pirosh found the ideal setting that would represent the desolation of the Siegfried Line, Hitler's last line of defense. Supplied with photographs, studio art directors began "designing" the look of the battlefield, complete with simulated concrete antitank "dragon's teeth," pillboxes and wrecked tanks. Simultaneously, a series of conferences and rehearsals were held with the young actors. Pirosh was immediately taken with McQueen.

"Steve was very stimulating to work with during the script stage," recalled Pirosh. "He was fun, and he had some terrific ideas which helped me develop the Reese character. He came up with little bits of dialogue and I though the guy was great. He was going to give a great performance and I was going to get some credit for it."

Although he admired McQueen and helped develop the Reese character into the film's major driving force, Pirosh still considered "Separation Hill" as a film, not unlike *Battleground*, about a group of soldiers, not a starring vehicle for any one actor.

But Steve McQueen's star was on the rise and he was tired of playing subordinate roles in films loaded with established name talent. Since "Separation Hill" featured a group of relatively unknown feature players and given the key role of Reese, McQueen saw the film as a major stepping stone in his march toward stardom.

Undaunted by Pirosh's desires, McQueen demanded that his part be built up. The writer/director stood his ground. Facing a decision similiar to John Sturges' on *The Great Escape* a year later, Rackin also went to his screenwriting bench, bringing in writer Richard Carr to rework the Reese character. In its potential for damaging his relationship with Pirosh, it was a dangerous move, but Rackin also did not want to lose McQueen.

Carr, who knew Pirosh through their mutual friend, John Cassavetes, was surprised to find himself working on the war script. "What they wanted," he recalled, "was an inexpensive writer. They were primarily concerned with the opening. McQueen felt, and I think rightfully so, that his character wasn't clearly

One of Steve McQueen's interesting early film roles was in Never So Few *(MGM, 1959), directed by John Sturges.*

defined and that there was no empathy for him. So I rewrote the opening after discussing it with Bob. It gave Reese an entrance. Whereas Bob had opened with him joining the unit in the field, I began the film in a village behind the lines. In this way, I simply introduced the characters in a more effective way. I didn't change them."

Pirosh accepted Carr's new opening and continued to prepare the unit for location shooting near Mount Shasta. Problems continued, though, with both Rackin and McQueen. With new script changes forthcoming and his relationship with the latter slowly deteriorating, Pirosh decided one afternoon in late May 1961 to drop the entire project. He was disgusted and he approached Rackin asking for his release.

"Marty, I've done the script and you've paid me. You also paid for my expenses in scouting the locations. But as far as directing the film, I'm through. I'm not getting along with McQueen. Cut off my salary right now!" Rackin's half-hearted plea for the director to reconsider was rejected and Pirosh left the office at Paramount, never to return.

With the prospect of production costs spiraling in the event of a delay, Rackin wasted little time finding a new director. He hired Don Siegel. During World War II, Siegel was in Hollywood directing short subjects, two of which won Oscars. He was an interesting contrast to Pirosh. When he read the "Separation Hill" script for the first time, he was immediately dismayed at the amount of humor in the story, and although he thought humor at times an excellent device, he couldn't see anything funny about the desperate situation depicted in the film. Like Carr, he too was shocked to learn that Pirosh had left the project.

"Pirosh was a personal friend of mine," he related, "and I told Marty Rackin how much I thought of Bob. He acknowledged my admiration, saying 'I too must have liked him or I wouldn't have given him the job, but I'm telling you right now that he's not going to do the picture. Somebody's going to, and if you don't I'll

---

Facing page: *Sergeant Pike (Fess Parker, center) orders his squad into action. Reese (McQueen) fires his modified submachine gun, Homer (Nick Adams) reloads, Corby (Bobby Darin) prepares to open fire.* — Hell Is for Heroes *(Paramount, 1962).*

get someone who will.' I told Rackin that I would have to talk to Bob first, but he told me to wait until the deal was set."

But Siegel didn't wait. He phoned his friend that night and gave it to him. "What the hell are you doing? Are you as big an idiot as I am? Why are you throwing this project away?"

Look, Don," Pirosh said, "I don't want to talk about it. I'm not getting along with either McQueen or Rackin."

"Rackin offered me the project, but I know it's your picture," said Siegel, "do you have any feelings about me taking over?"

Pirosh calmed down. "No, but thanks for asking. I'd just as soon have you direct than somebody I didn't know."

"At least," Siegel pleaded, 'why not carry on as producer, and certainly as the writer?"

"No thanks," said Pirosh, thinking of Carr already rewriting his script. In desperation, Siegel launched one last assault on Pirosh's pride.

"Bob I think you're making a very serious mistake. It isn't necessary to be a triple threat man. As long as you're having problems, let someone else come and direct. But don't desert the whole project!"

The assault failed. Siegel hung up and went to sleep. The next morning he called Rackin and accepted the directing assignment.

With a new director in charge, the script revisions took on a more serious turn. Siegel began to eliminate much of Pirosh's original humor. Henshaw's duck was cut out of the story, Corby, the Bobby Darin character, was given a fresh approach and new dialogue was added to several key scenes.

Carr later explained that the original characters were expertly drawn but lacked certain movements that would have explained their individual natures.

"For instance, James Coburn played Henshaw, a guy who fixes things, a mechanic. Coburn wanted to wear glasses and appear studious. So instead of just talking about what he did, at the beginning of the story we introduced him working underneath a truck. Larkin comes over and asks, 'Whose truck is that?" and Henshaw looks absentmindedly back at him, replying, 'I don't know Sergeant.' Now with a little scene like this, you could tell that he was a quiet, reserved sort of a guy. It was one of those pictures where there had to be little touches like that to build the character."

Carr also added a scene in the early part of the film featuring the film's only actress, Michelle Montau, as a seductive bartender. "The purpose of that scene," Carr explains, "was to show Reese breaking the rules. He disregards the standing order that the town bar is off limits. He was getting drunk because he was unhappy. Pike comes into the bar, doesn't necessarily reprimand Reese (because they're old friends and they respect one another), and tells him that the unit is moving back on the line.

"Suddenly, all the moroseness leaves Reese. He picks up a bottle, tucks it in his jacket, flips on his steel helmet, and goes back to the squad. His life now has purpose once more. It was an illuminating scene that established Reese's rebellious nature early in the story."

Director Don Siegel was coordinating the location work in Redding with an army of stuntmen and extras when word reached him that the title of the film had been changed. Since "Separation Hill" was now considered too similiar to *Pork Chop Hill*, a Korean war drama released by United Artists two years earlier, the title had been switched to *Hell Is for Heroes*, a typically commercial designation dreamed up by the New York publicity office of Paramount Pictures. But, as Siegel explained, there was an associaton between the title and theme.

" 'Hell is for heroes' means that the ones that are heroic wind up in hell, they lose their legs or their lives. They have nothing to gain by being heroes. It's an exercise in futility, and hell is for heroes when you're brave enough, depending on your point of view, or stupid enough to go and attack a pillbox like Reese did. Where else are you going to end up?"

To keep the film's budget under control (*Hell Is for Heroes* would eventually cost $2.5 million), Rackin brought in Henry Blanke to produce the film. Blanke was a financial genius, having enjoyed a strong producing career, particularly in the 1930's with such films as *Anthony Adverse, The Life of Emile Zola*, and *Jezebel*. He was expensive, but Rackin needed a professional to control the film's spiraling budget. Blanke took over financial control of the film on June 21, 1961, nine days after Siegel had begun principal photography.

Pirosh had originally planned to shoot the film in the snow of winter. It was supposed to be cold on the Siegfried Line. But with the script revisions and production delays, the crew did not arrive in Redding until the high summer, when temperatures soared to 117 degrees, giving rise to Siegel's belief that Redding was, indeed, "the hell hole of the world."

Since the actors were forced to wear their heavy issue GI uniforms, Siegel decided to shoot a major portion of the film at night. It was one of the director's best moves. Not only were the "troops" more comfortable but the film, itself, benefitted from the increased atmosphere of night action.

Aside from the terrible weather conditions and the potential dangers of shooting night battles with large quantities of explosives, Siegel was continuing to have script problems. Seldom has there been more controversy over the definition and general philosophy of one character. In Pirosh's original script, Reese was portrayed as what the writer referred to as a "cowboy," a guy who went looking for trouble. The part had been drawn from the writer's wartime diary.

While his unit was advancing in the Ardennes, it was joined by a young major, whom Pirosh later referred to as a "typical eager beaver." This was the major's introduction to combat and Pirosh relates how this young officer spotted some German tanks in a nearby field and decided on a suicidal attack.

"This major comes running up and asks, 'What's going on here? Who's in charge?' I told him that I was and that we were pinned down.

" 'Sergeant,' he told me, 'get this platoon moving so that we can get at those tanks!' Five minutes later the major was dead and two of my men were wounded. That was a cowboy. Who the hell did he think he was, anyway, trying to take on those tanks?"

In reworking the introduction of the Reese character, Richard Carr felt that he did not change the original portrait of the wayward soldier that Reese was. Pirosh disagrees, claiming that Reese suffered a shift in emphasis, particularly in his climactic assault on the German pillbox, in which he is killed.

Facing page: *James Coburn starred as Henshaw, a bookish fix-all who is handy with a flamethrower.* — Hell Is for Heroes *(Paramount, 1962).*

Says Pirosh, "For my money, it lost the authentic attitude of the GI. There was a tendency to glorify and go for spectacular effects. And in the end, Steve McQueen goes with that 'gangbusters' attitude. I had worked out that last scene differently. I used a technical advisor who helped me come up with the moves, how he could take the pillbox on his own, and what kind of demolition he could use. I worked out every detail of it but I didn't have him go in with that attitude."

Classifying Reese as a psychotic, something the critics later saw in the Steve McQueen character, was something that Richard Carr failed to agree with.

"In the film *War Hunt*," he says, "John Saxon portrayed a depraved killer who puts on black face and goes out alone to kill Koreans, cutting off their ears and bringing them back. The commanding officer knows he's a psycho, but he lets him continue because he's valuable. Now as I see it, Reese in *Hell Is for Heroes* was just a guy who probably couldn't make it on the outside and away from the Army and who had terrible feelings about going back to civilian life.

"In fact, when the men believed they were going back to civilian life, Reese is very morose about it. He only perks up when Pike says that they are going back on the line. Reese probably hoped for the battlefield commission he had once lost, so that he could go back as an officer.

"He was an off-center guy, a misfit, a killer, but not a psychopath. He got behind the lines and simply had nothing to do. Reese doesn't become heroic at the end, he's just being the most professional soldier there. The way he attempts to take the pillbox in the ill-fated night attack, by using Henshaw to shield him with the flamethrower, was strictly legitimate.

"Later during the dawn massed attack, when he throws the satchel charge into the pillbox, he immediately dashes for a foxhole. He doesn't expect to get hit. But then, once he is hit and dying, his whole aim is for revenge. He sees the Germans throw out the charge and he gets up with his last ounce of energy, grabs

---

Facing page: *The final assault on the German pillbox. The concrete antitank devices, part of the German Siegfried Line, failed to halt the American advance.* — Hell Is for Heroes *(Paramount, 1962).*

the charge and rolls inside with it. He's dead anyway, his insides are all shot up. I don't think that his action in the end is really inconsistent with his other actions all along, which are solely professional.

"He did take too many chances to be classified as a true professional. Who's to say that Larkin wasn't the better soldier? He knew how to take orders. Reese thrived on the danger of combat. But there is a line which a man crosses to become a psycho, and Reese never did cross that line."

To clarify the character of Reese, Siegel and Carr had originally worked out a scene, later cut, that takes place after the failure of the abortive night raid on the pillbox—during which both Henshaw (James Coburn) and Colinsky (Mike Kellin) are killed.

Says Carr, "Originally, we had planned that this would be the scene where Reese reveals his true character. Pike would come over and ask him, 'Were you right?' and Reese would respond with an illuminating speech."

"Unfortunately, it came out stilted. McQueen and I worked on the speech and we tried to cut it down. Finally, it was Steve's idea that there would be no explanation, just a simple, "How do I know!" And that carried a lot more impact than a bunch of words or phony Freudian explanations. In a situation like that a guy isn't going to start talking anyway."

Director Siegel, who today is respected as one of Hollywood's top directors and a master of creating the unusual out of the obvious, sees Reese as an emotionally tormented individual, especially after the disastrous night raid. "I don't see how you could possibly go about killing people and not be affected by it. All soldiers are psychotic in some sense of the word. Certainly, Reese wasn't above the horror of his particular situation. He had enough emotion to burst into tears when he returned from the raid, and this was the last thing in the world that you'd expect. He was about to desert but he stops, with tears in his eyes, realizing that he can't quit. His guilt over the death of two men was terrific. He had to stay and fight."

For the crying sequence, which was later edited out of the film, Siegel found it almost impossible to get Steve McQueen to cry. There was no simple way. He used onions to no avail. Finally, he slapped the actor as hard as he could in the face.

"After that," he recalls, "I wanted to be as far way as possible. Then, when he comes up in a closeup, you can see his tears and his anger.

"In making the film as realistic as possible, I found one way was to play Steve as a professional, a real pro who was surrounded by amateurs. Certainly, with our cast, which came from all walks of life in the entertainment world, there was hardly a professional aura, and that made Steve stand out all the more."

Hell Is for Heroes was completed in the late summer of 1961. Paramount released the film in early 1962. Critically and commercially overshadowed by the more technically ambitious war films of the day, *The Longest Day, The Guns of Navarone, Merrill's Marauders* and *PT 109, Hell Is for Heroes* was nonetheless a minor classic. Directed with style, it managed to sidestep spectacle for its own sake and emphasized performance and atmosphere, two factors that successfully dramatized an incident from Robert Pirosh's wartime diary, and served to elevate the combat film to a more sophisticated level of artistic achievement.

III

The New Heroes

Looking back into the era which followed the Vietnam War's escalation in the summer of 1964, the effects of the conflict on the quality and success of American combat films are clearly discernible. Author James Jones' *The Thin Red Line*, perhaps the finest combat novel of World War II, became a darkly flavored, sterile tale of warfare that failed to generate much interest. Despite young Keir Dullea's excellent protrayal of Private Don Doll, the picture was a failure. While World War II continued to provide the conventional background for the dwindling entries in the super-hero phenomenon (*The Dirty Dozen, Kelly's Heroes* and *Where Eagles Dare*), a new group of controversial military films appeared.

Dealing effectively, pointedly and thus controversially with the realities of a new age of warfare, the new films continued to castigate the military tradition, expanding immensely on the twisted picture painted a decade earlier in *From Here to Eternity*. One of the most typical films of the period was director Stanley Kubrick's satirical triumph, *Doctor Strangelove: or, How I Learned to Stop Worrying and Love the Bomb* (Columbia Pictures, 1964), which attacked both militarism and the A-Bomb reality with a blend of factual drama, sharp satirical comment and allegory. Primarily a comedy, *Dr. Strangelove* still represents a realistic scenario demonstrating the threat of nuclear aggression in a nightmare world of political, military and sexual psychosis. It is not surprising that the United States Air Force refused to offer Kubrick military cooperation, the result being that the entire film was completed in England.

192

Having suffered through a recent bout of impotency, U.S. Air Force General Jack D. Ripper, one of Kubrick's best characters (portrayed by actor Sterling Hayden), blames his loss of essence on the fluoridation of American drinking water, which he refers to as part of the postwar communist conspiracy. He plans revenge by initiating a nuclear wing attack against Russia. Preferring to die than submit to "red supremacy," Ripper orders his B-52's across their last safety barrier (a fail safe point) into Russian airspace.

Portrayed as the typical gutsy base commander of the World War II mold, Ripper carries a .50-caliber machine gun in his golf bag, talks through a perpetual cigar and has perfect respect and admiration for his command. He is really a monster with a marvelous array of deadly atomic toys at his disposal. Should one of his bombers drop a solitary bomb on a Russian target, a "doomsday device" will be triggered automatically, and a terrible super weapon developed behind the Iron Curtain will destroy the entire world.

Meanwhile, in Washington, D.C., we are introduced to U.S. Air Force Chief of Staff General Buck Turgidson (George C. Scott), who learns of Ripper's attack order from his bikini clad personal secretary. We meet Turgidson clad in Hawaiian bermudas. A nightmarish caricature of military brashness, Turgidson is the film's best drawn character. Another obsessive anti-communist, he advises President Merkin Muffley (Peter Sellers) to bolster the attack by launching a massive first strike against the Russians. After all, there is no way they can turn back Ripper's squadron without the secret code. And Ripper had just killed himself. Turgidson secretly admires Ripper's bravado and, constantly harping on his mistrust of the communists, antagonizes his superior, who is trying to negotiate with the Russians.

Eventually, when negotiations with Premier Kissoff over the hot line prove successful and the wing attack is recalled, it is discovered that one aircraft, disabled and flying below enemy radar, is still heading for its target. Asked whether the plane has a a chance of hitting its target, Turgidson bellows his admiration for the plane's design, a product of good old American ingenuity.

"Now if the pilot's good, see, I mean if he's really sharp, he can barrel that baby in so low. You ought to see it some time, Mr. President, a big plane like a 52, with jet exhausts, whew..."

NUCLEAR WARHEAD
HANDLE WITH CARE
Hi THERE!
USAF
NUCLEAR WARHEAD
HANDLE WITH CARE
DEAR JOHN

Aboard the bomber is airplane commander Major "King Kong (Slim Pickens), a symbol of the atomic age warrior whose survival is tied to the effectiveness of his machine. Given the "go" code by Ripper, Kong reaches down and pulls out a cowboy hat, places it squarely on his head and, to the tune of "When Johnny Comes Marching Home Again," prepares his men for "Nuclear combat toe to toe with the Rooskies."

When his plane is crippled by a Russian surface-to-air missile, Kong stubbornly refuses to admit defeat. He loses three engines, his radio, and a great deal of fuel, but remains faithful in his resolve to clobber the target for the "folks back home." When the nuclear warhead gets caught in the bomb bay, Kong leaves his seat to free the device. Over the Russian target, he cuts the last wire and then rides the bomb to his, and the world's, doom whooping like a 19th-century cowboy.

Before the world is ripped apart, the camera races back to the "war room" where top U.S. Defense Department mind, Dr. Strangelove, an ex-Nazi, discusses a strange survival plan whereby, in the event of nuclear destruction, subjects of intense sexual attractiveness will retire to a series of deep mine shafts, and with a ratio of ten females to every male, rebuild the country's population in 97 years.

Dr. Strangelove was a commercially successful film that established director Stanley Kubrick as one of America's top creative film makers. It was as gross a statement on the hazards of the nuclear age and the degeneration of the military as could be depicted at that time. However, there was enough truth in it to give the film serious power and meaning. It is said that the Turgidson character still haunts the military.

Only a year later, in 1965, Columbia Pictures released *The Bedford Incident*, which carried the military reexamination a step further, dealing with a nuclear missile equipped destroyer tracking a Russian submarine in the North Atlantic. Captain Eric Finlander (Richard Widmark), a tough naval officer of the World War II mold, is obsessed with tracking down the encroaching submarine,

---

Facing page: *Major King Kong (Slim Pickens) about to make fateful ride.* — Dr. Strangelove *(Columbia, 1964).*

and his resultant obsession becomes a personal war that leads to another nuclear holocaust.

Attached to Finlander's destroyer, the *U.S.S. Bedford*, is liberal correspondent Ben Munsford (Sidney Poitier) who questions Finlander's strategy, and through whose eyes we appraise a Captain Queeg of the Atom Age. Like Ripper in *Dr. Strangelove*, Finlander's bravado is no longer practical.

His relentless pressure for efficiency cripples young Ensign Ralston (James MacArthur) who soon develops a chronic case of nerves. If such a relationship had developed during World War II, as it did in such films as *The Enemy Below* and *Run Silent, Run Deep*, the captain would have instilled courage and individual spirit in his nervous subaltern, and both would have turned their anxieties towards the enemy. But aboard the nuclear destroyer *Bedford,* such tension is no longer allowed such an outlet.

In the film's apocalyptic ending, Finlander instructs Munsford in the deployment of the *Bedford's* missile system. Ralston misinterprets the drill as an attack command and launches a nuclear strike which obliterates the Russian submarine. In turn, the *Bedford* is eliminated by a spread of atomic torpedoes that were fired just before the submarine was hit.

Films like *The Bedford Incident* portray the military at the mercy of their machines. Handcuffed by the demands of an age that continually preached prudence to fighting men, military leaders with World War II experience found themselves unable to deal rationally with their assignments. They failed to understand the meaning of the Cold War and the need for maintaining the peace. Such weakness proved devastating.

In *Seven Days in May* (Paramount Pictures, 1964), the film adaptation of the Fletcher Knebel novel, U.S. Air Force General James Scott (Burt Lancaster) dismisses President Jordan Lyman's (Fredric March) nuclear treaty with the Russians as "an act of criminal negligence" and plans a military takeover of the United States. Scott, another veteran of the Second World War thrust into the world of Cold War power politics and inaction, a man of combat by all its definitions, puts no faith in papers, especially when he is dealing with a country like Russia, which he claims, "has never honored a treaty in its entire history."

Richard Widmark (left) plays tough modern naval officer Eric Findlander, here listening to young Ensign Ralston (James MacArthur) shortly before The Bedford Incident *(Columbia, 1965).*

Scott symbolizes the basic military strategy that the only good defense is a viable offense. That the world is to survive under a perpetual threat of nuclear war is a situation the General deems inevitable.

The general's aide, Marine Colonel "Jiggs" Casey (Kirk Douglas) is a more modern warrior. Having stumbled upon his superior's plot, Casey contacts the President and actively participates in Lyman's countermeasures. Still, he holds the deepest respect for and even defends Scott until it is finally proven that his general is indeed immersed in treason. When one of the President's advisors castigates Scott as "a jackal," Casey explodes in anger, prompting Lyman's closing speech which chastizes, not the conspirators, but the age of insecurity that produced their conspiracy. The clearly defined realities of World War II had vanished, and it is through Lyman's eyes that we begin to see the true enemy.

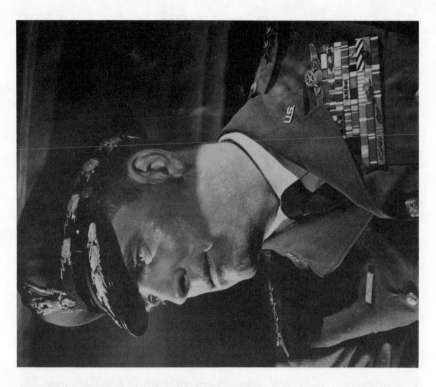

As the war in Vietnam continued, other factors affected the portrayal of combat on the screen. To make up for the loss of such a violent and adventuresome genre, Hollywood suddenly and graphically transferred mass bloodshed to more conventional films such as the Western and police drama. The killing machines were being reprogrammed. The tough soldier was replaced by the tough cop. Ironically, in the new police dramas, many of these men were Vietnam veterans. Dope smugglers, early 20th-century Mexican banditos, and the Mafia substituted often for the conventional enemies of World War II. It was the reversal of the phenomenon of the later 1930's when Hollywood abandoned its war on crime and corruption and geared instead for the conflict against fascism.

Further hindering the creative push towards more World War II combat films, was the conspicuous absence of equipment. The ordnance sought exhaustively by Darryl F. Zanuck at the beginning of the decade had once again vanished. Without a source of free battle hardware, it was impossible even to consider the combat film as a creative alternative.

Two vital factors combined to provide the means for a breakthrough. Even as American troops mired themselves in the rice-paddy war, a young screenwriter named Francis Ford Coppola, barely out of college, was writing a new, highly unusual, military screenplay, while half way across the world, producer Frank McCarthy discovered a treasure trove of usable military hardware. In 1970, these factors united in a cinematic triumph entitled *Patton*. With such forces at work the final synthesis had arrived.

Facing page, left: *Kirk Douglas as Colonel "Jiggs" Casey, the modern warrior;* right: *Burt Lancaster as General James Scott, the anachronism.* —Seven Days in May (*Paramount, 1964*).

8

The Final Synthesis

I want you to remember that no bastard ever won a war by dying for his country. He won it, by making the other poor dumb bastard die for his country! — George C. Scott as *Patton* (1970).

So elaborately staged and yet so undeniably realistic, writer Francis Ford Coppola's pre-credits soliloquy, culled from General George S. Patton's wartime speeches to his men, was merely the opening introduction to a complex character study which brought to a successful conclusion the long war against a prohibitive censorship code that forbid men of war to say what they felt on screen.

Draped behind the imposing figure of Patton (George C. Scott, in an Oscar winning role) was a giant replica of the Stars and Stripes. The American warrior was exquisitely manicured, down to the shine on his pearl-handled revolvers, and his profanities and expletives, delivered in a raspy tirade, instead of being an affront, demonstrated instead the General's overall sense of direction and supreme confidence. It was all a carefully planned, and flawlessly executed paradox.

In 1970, during the height of the Vietnam War, at a time when militarism was the dirtiest of all possible words, when the government of the United States and the Pentagon were the targets of a great swell of organized, outspoken and frequently violent criticism from all levels of society, when the motion picture industry shunned practically all World War II combat films as

200

totally unmarketable, 20th Century-Fox, the studio that had once gambled its reserves on Darryl F. Zanuck's *The Longest Day*, gambled another $12 million on a mammoth screen dramatization of one of World War II's most controversial field commanders.

And, yet, was it really a gamble at all? In 1948, MGM executive Dore Schary had defended his film, *Battleground*, by maintaining that story and not topic was the deciding factor. Twenty years later, Fox producer Frank McCarthy voiced similar sentiments. He had a screenplay that could surmount the enormous wave of anti-militarism and unite a divided audience in a fascinating character experience. He also had George C. Scott, perhaps America's finest actor.

The traditional combat film format was abandoned with *Patton* and instead the unusual motivation and fate of military history's most controversial character was revealed. Like his nemesis in the Tunisian desert, Rommel, "the Desert Fox," Patton was a fighting general, a master of movement and tactics. He was also a competent poet, a vivid writer, a student of history, and a very religious man who strongly believed in reincarnation.

The film version of his military career begins shortly after the American landings in North Africa in November 1942 and ends shortly before Patton's death in a German automobile accident in December 1945. A triumph of historical drama and objectivity, *Patton* presented a tapestry of moods, emotions and visions of war as seen through the General's eyes, a portrait that allowed the audience to form its own judgment of the character's actions.

Thus, *Patton* became a mirror through which warring doves and hawks viewed the confirmation of their own deeply emotional beliefs. To the former, General Patton was the anti-Christ, who symbolized the gutsy brand of militarism that had led to the Vietnam debacle. And yet, as an audience, they found it difficult to criticize a film that was so overtly honest. It would be the key to the film's success, for there was no need to embellish or disparage the character of Patton, the paradox of his makeup was obvious from the beginning.

To the hawks, *Patton* offered a nostalgic look at a simple time, a period when super heroes were also super patriots and when victory was made possible through military action. With his earthy vocabulary and dashing leadership, Patton personified to them a kind of man the absence of whom was a major factor in the Vietnam War. In essence, he symbolized their impossible dream. At the same time, they could not deny the offensiveness of the man's profanity, his lack of any vestige of courtesy and his pompous demand for military protocol and correctness, even in the front lines.

Even while the film pleased ideological extremists, it also appealed to the discriminating entertainment seeking viewer. As Patton, actor George C. Scott met their equally demanding standards magnificently, and despite the grandeur of the production, one never lost sight of the principle focus.

A product of the new generation of actors, Scott influenced every scene, every action. He was well suited to the demanding role, for he lacked the stigma of superstardom, an established image that might have neutralized the effectiveness of his characterization. Throughout the film, he remained the complex historical figure, faithfully depicting every mannerism and every insult.

Darryl F. Zanuck was the patriarchal war horse of 20th Century-Fox. Now chairman of the board, he persuaded his fellow board members and his son, Richard (head of production) that producer Frank McCarthy's *Patton* project was feasible and potentially valuable. With pleasant memories of *The Longest Day* and his talent for thoroughness, Zanuck began to lay the groundwork for potential military cooperation.

It was retired Brigadier General Frank McCarthy's memo to Darryl Zanuck, dated October 23, 1951, that originally initiated the idea of a film about America's colorful wartime hero. Such a project was made possible by the death of General Patton's widow, a woman who had vehemently opposed a film dramatization of her husband's life. In 1951, McCarthy urged his superior to consider the *Patton* project and all its apparent possibilities. But, for 13 years, he was denied Pentagon assistance because two of Patton's children were in or directly tied to the service (Patton's son was an Army officer and his daughter was married to a soldier).

"And then," relates McCarthy (who would later come to dramatize the life of General Douglas MacArthur in a 1977 film), "after many years it occurred to me that we might make the picture in Spain. At the end of World War II, we needed airfields in the Mediterranean, and the Spaniards, with a very poorly equipped army, decided to trade us the airfields we needed for surplus military hardware. They got tanks, aircraft, modes of transportation, rifles and artillery. Spain remained poor and they were not soon able to replace the surplus material with more modern equipment. By 1969, when we went on location for *Patton* the Spaniards still had everything and we were able to rent their entire army for the film."

Both former Signal Corps Colonel Darryl Zanuck and retired General McCarthy were fascinated by the project's creative potential, and they were able to transfer their enthusiasm to the rest of the 20th Century-Fox board. Fox was in much better straits than it had been in the early 1960's. Films like *The Sound of Music,* and *Planet of the Apes* had seen to that. Given such a secure foundation, the Fox executives were willing to invest $12 million in *Patton.*

Zanuck spelled out his feeling for the subject in a detailed memorandum sent to his son in February 1966. "Personally, I look upon him as a great man. I think he was correct in kicking his soldiers in the ass. I think he was right in wanting to use ex-Nazis as German administrators in Bavaria. I am not sure if he was entirely wrong about taking on the Russians at the River Elbe. I admire him and believe in most instances that he was absolutely right. I wonder, however, if American audiences will understand, especially in these times, or appreciate him as much as I do. Perhaps this will provide the contoversy we want in the picture."

McCarthy was also convinced that an honest character study could transcend the film's obvious military format. "Darryl and I believed that this was to be a story of a man of World War II. It didn't relate whatsoever to Vietnam. We were dealing with history and to many to today's young people, World War II is ancient history, just as the Civil War was remote to me when I was a youngster growing up with two grandfathers who had fought for the Confederacy."

Gut level enthusiasm aside, it was young Francis Ford Coppola's intriguing first draft screenplay that convinced everyone, including actor George C. Scott, that *Patton* was indeed a practical undertaking. Only 26, Coppola was something of a phenomenon in Hollywood. The son of a classical flautist, Francis was born in Detroit, on April 7, 1939. He was barely 5 when Patton's Third Army crossed France and raced for the German border.

At 8 he was already tinkering with the family 8mm projector, and two years later, during a painful bout with polio, he fitted home-made soundtracks to silent 16mm films. Later, at Hofstra University on Long Island, New York, he wrote and directed several musicals, and in 1962 at UCLA won the Samuel Goldwyn Award for a hastily written screenplay.

In 1964, the shrewd bearded film maker was already a veteran of the Hollywood wars. Fighting his battles in the cutting room while fellow film students debated Eisenstein and Renoir, Coppola was already writing and selling screenplays to Warner Brothers (11 in two years) when he was assigned to his first military project, the film dramatization of the Larry Collins/Dominique Lapierre novel, *Is Paris Burning?* — a baptism of fire which became a political nightmare.

Assigned to dramatize a fascinating leftist uprising against the retreating Nazis in occupied Paris, Coppola was instead restrained by a series of political maneuvers, which eventually diluted the entire impact of the story. The months spent in Paris with cowriter Gore Vidal, director René Clement and two French scenarists, were enlightening, if nothing else.

Recalls Coppola, "For some stupid reason, Clement's contract didn't give him a say over the script and for some equally stupid reason, the producer wanted to keep it that way. So to circumvent this, Clement's ideas were presented as mine at story conferences, and of course I didn't mind, since Clement's ideas invariably were the best.

"In any case, they were all terrified. They wouldn't even admit that there were any communists in France during the war. Or, if there were, we were never to use their names. The de Gaulle regime didn't acknowledge their existence then or now. The whole essence of the plot was the battle between the communists and the Gaullists for control of the city. And if we couldn't have that, I couldn't see where there was a movie."

Convinced by Vidal that they could overcome their difficulties, Coppola controlled his frustration, finished the script, and happily left Paris. Despite location shooting, and an all-star international cast (including Kirk Douglas as General Patton), *Is Paris Burning?* became one of the most disappointing films in 1966.

Coppola's film savvy impressed Frank McCarthy immediately. He was searching for a young, disciplined writer who would bring no preconceived ideas to the *Patton* project. The producer desired such a scribe to dive into his painstakingly assembled research materials, and surface with an entirely fresh perspective. Ironically, Coppola's problems on *Is Paris Burning?* not only won him the *Patton* project but they prepared him for the political demands of the new script. Politics and creativity are strange bedfellows in the motion picture business, and Coppola suffered through enough sleepless Parisian nights to understand the complex tightrope he would soon walk.

On a cool, clear spring morning in 1965, Coppola arrived at General McCarthy's campaign tent (actually an air conditioned office at the Westwood Fox lot) and was issued his field equipment. Assigned to him were no fewer than 12 biographies of Patton, including the most comprehensive, author Ladislas Farago's *Ordeal and Triumph*, which the studio had just purchased. He also received a packet of research materials prepared by Robert S. Allen, a syndicated columist, who had served with the Intelligence division of Patton's Third Army.

On that very night he conceived of the film's opening scene, the long illuminatory prologue sequence in which a bemedaled Patton addresses his troops before an immense American flag. Coppola was experienced enough to realize that a film of this nature needed an opening of sheer shock value, evocative of the film's central theme. Coppola believed that Patton was at his most colorful while addressing the men under his command. He became their military leader, their father, their priest and their god. He believed strongly in the gut level appeal to his men on the eve of battle.

Patton cursed, joked, related anecdotes of courage and impressed his men with a strong fighting resolve. Their immediate superiors enlightened them as to the where and when, he instructed them in the more important why. Like Attila the Hun, Patton appeared above them on a raised platform as the "scourge of God,"

"Gaudy as a peacock" was how Director Coppola described General Patton (George C. Scott) in the carefully planned opening scene address to the troops. — Patton *(20th Century-Fox, 1970).*

and still his speeches were warmly appreciated. The men of the United States Third Army strongly felt that they were the finest combat troops in the world. It was this type of indoctrination that would contribute to their great success in battle.

Coppola also felt that it was important to create the proper setting for the speech. He formulated the paradox of having a vast American flag draped behind the General, and Patton would appear in his dressiest garb. The prologue would set the pace and theme for the entire film. The speech itself was completely authentic, much of it drawn from the General's wartime speeches. Coppola searched for revealing phrases, and profanity was included indiscriminately. It was the age of the new morality and soldiers were able to speak naturally for the first time:

> "Now, an army is a team. This individuality stuff is a lot of crap. The bilious bastards who wrote that stuff about individuality for the *Saturday Evening Post* don't know anymore about real battle than they do about fornicating!"

George S. Patton was most colorful when revealing his basic military strategy and his obsession with movement. More than any general in history, Patton symbolized the birth of armored warfare, and the death of static defense.

> I don't want to get any messages saying, "We are holding our position." We're not holding anything. Let the Hun do that. We are advancing constantly and are not interested in holding onto anything except the enemy. We're going to hold onto him by the nose and kick him in the ass. We'll kick the hell out of him all the time and we'll go through him like crap through a goose!

Patton always concluded his speeches with a special brand of poignancy:

> There's one thing you men will be able to say when you get home and you may all thank God for it. Thirty years from now when you are sitting around the fireside with your grandson on your knee and he asks what you did in the great World War II, you won't have to say, "Well, I shoveled shit in Louisiana."

Director George Seaton who was present at the film's 1970 premiere, recalled the audience's reaction to the opening prologue: "There were hisses and boos when the curtain went up and everyone saw the American flag draped across the entire screen. But this attitude was slowly altered by the texture and candor of

the speech, until, at the very end, the 'shoveling shit in Louisiana' line broke up the entire audience. Everyone laughed, and it was a wonderful touch that gave the film an immediate anti-war feeling."

In his first draft screenplay, Coppola revealed General Patton's vision of himself as a reincarnated warrior, the classic military leader destined to lead the Allied armies to victory against the Hun. As such, he saw war, battle and death in the classical sense. To convert this vision to the screen, Coppola frequently prefaced many of his scenes with descriptive phrases that would aid both the director and the cinematographer in deciding what technical effects they could use to recreate Patton's moody concept of war. Before the climactic Battle of El Guettar, where Patton's II Corps defeated Rommel's 10th Panzer Division, Coppola writes, "The sun begins its roast of the desert sand. The music is dissonant and ancient as though the battlefield is strangely eternal...."

Coppola was also deeply aware of symbolism and how it could help reveal Patton's inner character. He reasoned that careful attention should be paid to the General's appearance and that every mannerism should be carefully used by the actor playing the role.

Coppola's 202 page first draft roughly follows the Farago book, covering the General's involvement in World War II, without going into his life before the war. Much of the dramatic conflict in the screenplay is provided by the relationship between Patton and his subordinate in North Africa, and later superior in Western Europe, General Omar Bradley. Remarked McCarthy in a story conferences with Coppola, "The steadfastness, sanity and calm of Bradley accentuates the flamboyancy and rashness of Patton, although we do not lose sight of the fact that both men are magnificent soldiers. The more we strengthen Bradley, the better will be the contrast between the two."

Like the Harvey Stovall character in *Twelve O'Clock High*, we see much of the action in "Patton" over Bradley's shoulders. This is a war of movement, grand decisions, high level strategy and personality clashes. Battle is seen once again, from a distance.

Facing page: *Patton (George C. Scott) acknowledges the salute of a group of Arab youngsters en route to his new command in North Africa.* — Patton *(20th Century-Fox, 1970).*

Coppola added another perspective on his own by creating scenes behind German lines at the Reichschancellory in Berlin where the enemy's reaction to Patton's success is gauged. General Alfred Jodl assigns a former professor of literature named Captain Steiger to compile a complete dossier on Patton, and it is through such a device that we learn additional factors about Patton before the war. His functional belief in the lessons of military history leads Steiger to believe that Patton will follow the Athenian example and invade Sicily after his success in North Africa.

Despite his scripts' unusual format and brilliant pace, Coppola's first draft lacked a certian cohesiveness. In McCarthy's words, "it was like having a handful of pearls and no string." Coppola turned in his first draft on New Year's Eve 1965 and, with a new bankroll, began preparing two new films. One of them, *You're a Big Boy Now* was to become the dramatization of his master's thesis at UCLA.

While telegrams sailed back and forth between McCarthy and the Zanucks, appraising the script, preparing for the film's military cooperation and gauging the cost of the Spanish Army, a director was sought to take over the production. Everyone's immediate choice was William Wyler, a good friend of McCarthy's.

Unfortunately, Wyler disliked the Coppola script. He failed to see the writer's objective viewpoint. And Wyler, who was forever making profound and deeply significant motion pictures, desired a more concrete approach to the mysterious Patton. Coppola had developed the General through his wartime experiences which provided a structuralized plot. Wyler was far more interested in the General's background and the factors that contributed to his unusual behavior.

In the early spring of 1966, Wyler confronted McCarthy, "Frank, we ought to start over and get Jim Webb to do the script. He was with Patton in North Africa. I know he'll do a wonderful job."

Facing page: *Gregory Peck starred as Lt. Joe Clemens in the highly acclaimed Korean War drama* Pork Chop Hill *(United Artists, 1959), directed by Lewis Milestone and written by Sy Bartlett and James Ruffin Webb.*

McCarthy objected. Plans were already being finalized to do this film in Spain that very summer. To junk Coppola's unpolished screenplay and begin anew was madness, so Wyler backed out and McCarthy tried to interest another director, a difficult chore because the Zanucks were obviously looking for a good investment. Between prior commitments, executive preference, and just plain apathy to the project, McCarthy could find no one.

While correspondence with the Spanish military resumed, the shooting date was postponed. Since everyone respected Wyler's creative savvy and alternative directors were definitely lacking, Richard Zanuck gave McCarthy the authority to assign Webb to the project.

First Lieutenant James Ruffin Webb was attached to II Corps in North Africa when George Patton replaced General Lloyd R. Fredendall after the disastrous battle of the Kasserine Pass. Throughout the remainder of the African campaign, Webb observed the colorful Patton in his native habitat. Webb knew Patton, and this had convinced Wyler that he was the perfect writer for the project.

A premiere constructionist, Webb was one of Hollywood's most respected writers, a veritable master at dramatizing American history. He had won an Academy Award in 1963 for his multifaceted screenplay for *How the West Was Won*, and his other works included the post-Civil War story *Vera Cruz* (1954), the unusual tale of early American Indian life in *Kings of the Sun* (1963), the classic Korean War drama *Pork Chop Hill* (1959) and the complex western *Cheyenne Autumn* (1964).

A stickler for detail and accuracy, Webb began researching anew and it was not until the winter of 1966-1967 that he was ready to begin a script. Meanwhile, McCarthy had secured the help of Omar Bradley who agreed to read and annotate the final screenplay.

Webb's script also begins in North Africa in 1942, but during the course of the story, it flashes back to the General's earlier life before the war. Preliminary scenes showed Patton in Mexico, chasing Pancho Villa with General Pershing, playing polo in Hawaii (to the consternation of General Drum), demonstrating armored tactics and equipment during the Louisiana maneuvers of

1941, and much of his early life as a young aristocrat growing up in Pasadena, California.

Webb also treated Patton's campaigns in a more detailed and professional manner. He discussed behind the scenes strategy, and many of the scenes were portrayed as if taken right out of the official campaign summaries. Dealing professionally with a topic that held a special appeal for him, Webb's final script was a cohesive tribute to the wayward life of Patton. But as McCarthy soon put it, "It was a beautifully structured script but the pearls had disappeared and now I had the string."

At a time when even the most controversial strategem lacked any intrinsic fascination, Webb had concentrated on the General's battlefield savvy, failing to emphasize the unique mystery of the reincarnate. Still, Wyler was happy with the script, as it delved expertly into the General's background. On this basis, McCarthy began searching for an actor to play Patton. In one of the most frustrating casting searches in film history, he was turned down by almost every major actor in Hollywood. Even George C. Scott who had been interested in the project from the beginning declined the offer based on the new Webb material.

"Most of the actors," recalled McCarthy, were simply afraid of the Webb script, because they thought it was too much of a glorification. I was afraid of this, but I was also convinced that Wyler could turn such interesting material into a beautiful film."

Further complicating George C. Scott's interest in the project was Wyler himself, who had recently fired him off the set of *How to Steal a Million*. In the spring of 1968, Wyler announced his own departure. Partially deaf, and no longer at his physical peak, he was now convinced that the rigors of filming outdoors in a multiplicity of Spanish locations and climates would prove too arduous. It was a difficult decision, for Wyler was quite taken with his subject.

McCarthy felt beaten. After three years of concentrated effort, he possessed two unworkable scripts, no director and no star. It appeared as if General Patton had lost his greatest battle. There were, fortunately, other good forces at work. On June 12, 1968, Fox producer David Brown was lunching in New York when he was approached by George C. Scott's agent, Jane Deacy. Brown expressed his regret over Wyler's departure which prompted her to say that Scott was still interested in the project if McCarthy would return to the original Coppola material.

Brown cabled McCarthy that very same day. Jolted from his doldrums, the producer signed Scott with assurances, dusted off the Coppola script and called in veteran screenwriter Edmund North to string the pearls.

With General Bradley as a functioning mine of information, North, who later shared Academy Award credit with Coppola (a man he never met), tightened the script, adding anecdotes, some of which were supplied by Patton's daughter. Building the Bradley character into an important force in the film prompted the studio to purchase the General's autobiography, *A Soldier's Story*.

Another expert constructionist, North had dealt with complex military strategy, albeit waterborne, in 1959 on the *Sink the Bismarck* project, also for 20th Century-Fox. As North worked diligently on the final polish, McCarthy searched once more for a director who, like Coppola, could approach the subject objectively and with a firm hand.

At that time, the 20th Century-Fox lot was teeming with characters from an ambitious new science fiction film based on French author Pierre Boulle's novel, *Planet of the Apes*. Directing the army of Simian soldiers was Franklin Schaffner. McCarthy knew Schaffner's work and was impressed with the realistic medieval battle scenes he had filmed for *The War Lord* three years earlier.

No mere director of movement, Schaffner had an experienced eye for performance. In 1964, the year of the political thriller, he had directed the film adaptation of Gore Vidal's play, *The Best Man*, a fascinating study of political intrigue that would raise not a few eyebrows in Hollywood. In later films such as *Papillon, Islands in the Stream,* and *The Boys from Brazil,* Schaffner would demonstrate his adeptness at filling the screen with sweeping adventure and three dimensional characters. He was a new breed of director.

Impressed with his vitality and versatility, McCarthy signed Schaffner to the *Patton* project. It was a bold and decisive move that eventually paid off handsomely. Schaffner took to battle sequences naturally, and with his mind constantly a maze of logistics, he would be at home in Spain during the spring of 1969.

From the snow of Segovia (simulating snowy Bastogne during the Battle of the Bulge) to the sand and scrub of Almeria (simulating the sandy wastes of Tunisia), Schaffner and his ace cinematographer Fred Koenekamp, created the proper tapestry of moods, visions and actions.

* * *

The hour is late, the house is silent, except for one room where the steady clickety-click of a motion picture projector can be heard. Surrounded by empty beer cans, his head resting against a sofa, his knees drawn up to his chest, George C. Scott watches a silent film intently. Piled beside him is a stack of archaic film cannisters with official U.S. Army titles. As one reel is completed, he replaces it with another. The projector once more clicks to life as we see the title, "Patton arrives in Sicily."

We see a landing craft approaching a beach. The ramp drops down and General George S. Patton, Jr., steps triumphantly onto Sicilian soil. Scott studies Patton, alert for the characteristic mannerisms, the General's walk, his posture, his facial expressions, the cut of his uniform, the reaction of his subordinates. Nothing escapes his trained eye. Having studied this man constantly for six months, preparing himself mentally for all of the General's complexities, Scott is now undergoing phase number two of his indoctrination — the physical transformation.

Says Scott, "One has to use one's body to try to get the most penetrating habits and characteristics. In the case of General Patton, it was his carriage. I have never seen him slouch. He was an erect human being. I'm sure he slept straight. I can't picture him in a fetal position, even as a child. He was also a publicly emotional person who would cry at the sight of green grass. His emotions were always close to the surface."

The documentary film continues as Patton greets his victorious Corps commanders and strides toward a jeep that will take him further inland. Despite his fatigue, Scott's eyes never falter. It is 1969. Twenty-four years have passed since the end of World War II. But the fascination has not withered. In the living room of a Beverly Hills mansion, the final synthesis of American combat films is being professionally nurtured over warm beer.

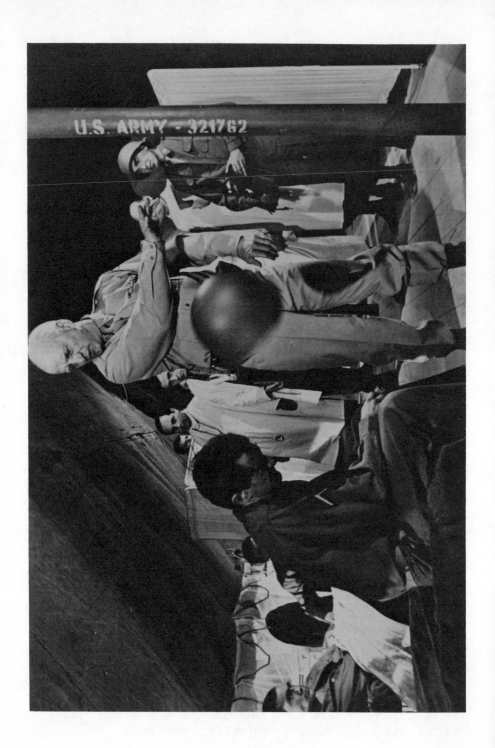

* * *

It is May Day in Madrid. "Patton" is nearly finished. There is only one more scene to be shot. On the northern wall of a vast soundstage, a huge American flag has been tacked professionally. Fred Koenekamp places his cameras expertly and the crew waits expectantly for the "General's" arrival. At precisely 12:00 noon, George C. Scott steps onto the platform.

With his head shaved and dyed white, his nose reshaped and his jaw lengthened, he has become Patton, a perfect replica created out of the magic kit of the makeup and wardrobe department. But the transformation is more than physical.

Scott walks steadily and erect, his chest thrown out, his head upright, his eyes on fire. In a raspy voice he informs Schaffner that he is ready. The lights dim and the camera sweeps the stage. McCarthy, who is standing next to Schaffner, whispers his approval.

For a moment, Scott stands quietly, majestically. Absolute stillness prevails over the large stage as he begins to speak. As the crew listens and watches in fascination, Scott disappears before their eyes and Patton emerges. The General has reincarnated once again.

The speech is given in one flawless take and Schaffner yells, "Cut!"

Magic lingers for a another moment before the crew breaks into great and spontaneous applause. Once more the actor, Scott smiles, acknowledges their plaudits with a polite nod and walks off the set.

When it was released *Patton* succeeded in uniting a badly fragmented audience disgusted with the debacle of Vietnam. The critical and commercial success of the film proved that the fascination with World War II, with its characters, battles, atmosphere and courage, was far from over.

Facing page: *The slap heard round the world — when General Patton (Scott) slapped a nerve-wracked soldier in Sicily and lost his command.* — Patton *(20th Century-Fox, 1970).*

"Always audacious, always audacious," was perhaps Patton's best motto. Here he (Scott) confronts a map of Europe prior to the June 1944 Allied invasion. — Patton *(20th Century-Fox, 1970).*

The films are more professional now. Men like Darryl F. Zanuck, Sam Spiegel, John Sturges, and Robert Pirosh saw to that. The grueling production difficulties remain, but they only provide a continuing challenge to the film makers of the future.

In their own special way, the combat films of World War II have contributed to the fulfillment of D.W. Griffith's 1912 prophecy that the motion picture could eventually teach effective world history. Thirty years of sweat and controversy have gone into the making of films of the combat genre. The glory has faded, but historical interest will continue to fan the embers of creative fire, resulting in ever-improving films and a more perceptive look into our military past.

Appendix
Cast and Technical Credits

A Walk in the Sun (20th Century-Fox, 1945)

Producer Lewis Milestone. *Director* Lewis Milestone. *Screenplay by* Robert Rossen, *based on a story by* Harry Brown. *Director of photography* Russel Harlan. *Musical score* Frederic Efrem Rich. *Ballads — Lyrics* Millard Lampell; *Music* Earl Robinson. *Art direction by* Max Bertisch. *Film editor* Duncan Mansfield. *Sound by* Corson Jewett. *Assistant director* Maurie Suess. *Production manager* Joseph H. Nadel. *Technical advisor* Col. Thomas D. Drake.

Cast: *Sgt. Tyne* Dana Andrews. *Rivera* Richard Conte. *Windy* John Ireland. *Friedman* George Tyne. *Sgt. Ward* Lloyd Bridges. *Mc-Williams* Sterling Holloway. *Sgt. Porter* Herb Rudley. *Archimbeau* Norman Lloyd. *Judson* Steve Brodie. *Carraway* Huntz Hall. *Sgt. Hoskins* James Cardwell. *Rankin* Chris Drake. *Tranella* Richard Benedict. *Tinker* George Offerman, Jr. *Trasker* Danny Desmond. *Cousins* Victor Cutler. *Giorgio* Anthony Dante. *Cpl. Kramer* Harry Cline.

Battleground (MGM, 1949)

Producer Dore Schary. *Director* William A. Wellman. *Screenplay by* Robert Pirosh, and *story by* Robert Pirosh. *Director of photography* Paul C. Vogel. *Music by* Lennie Hayton. *Art direction by* Cedric Gibbons and Hans Peters. *Set decorations by* Edwin B. Willis and Alfred E. Spencer. *Film editor* John Dunning. *Sound by* Douglas Shearer. *Makeup by* Jack Dawn. *Montage sequences by* Peter Ballbusch. *Technical advisor* H. W. O. Kinnard.

Cast: *Holley* Van Johnson. *Jarvess* John Hodiak. *Rodriguez* Ricardo Montalban. *"Pop" (Ernest J. S. Stazak)* George Murphy. *Jim Layton* Marshall Thompson. *Abner Spudler* Jerome Courtland. *Standiferd* Don Taylor. *Wolowicz* Bruce Cowling. *Kinnie* James Whitmore. *"Kipp" Kippton* Douglas Fowley. *Chaplain* Leon Ames. *Hanson* Guy Anderson. *Doc ("Medic")* Thomas E. Breen. *Denise* Denise Darcel. *Bettis* Richard Jaeckel. *Garby* Jim Arness. *William J. Hooper* Scotty Beckett. *Lt. Teiss* Brett King.

Twelve O'Clock High (20th Century-Fox, 1949)

Producer Darryl F. Zanuck. *Director* Henry King. *Screenplay by* Sy Bartlett and Beirne Lay, Jr., *based on the novel by* Beirne Lay, Jr., and Sy Bartlett. *Director of photography* Leon Shamroy. *Special photographic effects by* Fred Sersen. *Music by* Alfred Newman. *Art direction by* Lyle Wheeler and Maurice Ransford. *Set decoration by* Thomas Little and Bruce Macdonald. *Film editor* Barbara McLean. *Sound by* W. D. Flick and Roger Heman. *Makeup artist* Ben Nye. *Orchestration* Edward Powell. *Air Force technical advisor* Col. John H. de Russy, 305th Bombing Group, Chelveston, England, 1942.

Cast: *Gen. Savage* Gregory Peck. *Lt. Col. Ben Gately* Hugh Marlowe. *Col. Davenport* Gary Merrill. *Gen. Pritchard* Millard Mitchell. *Maj. Stovall* Dean Jagger. *Sgt. McIllhenny* Robert Arthur. *Capt. "Doc" Kaiser* Paul Stewart. *Maj. Cobb* John Kellogg. *Lt. Bishop* Bob Patten. *Nurse* Joyce MacKenzie. *Lt. Wilson* Don Hicks. *Lt. Zimmerman* Lee MacGregor. *Birdwell* Sam Edwards. *Interrogation officer* Roger Anderson. *Sgt. Ernie* John Zilly. *Lt. Pettinghill* William Short. *Lt. McKessen* Richard Anderson. *Capt. Twombley* Lawrence Dobkin. *Sentry* Kenneth Tobey. *Operations officer* John McKee. *Mr. Britton* Campbell Copelin. *Dwight* Don Guadagno. *Weather observer* Peter Ortiz. *Clerk in antique shop* Steve Clark. *Clerk* Pat Whyte.

The Bridge on the River Kwai (Columbia, 1957)

Producer Sam Spiegel. *Director* David Lean. *Screenplay by* Pierre Boulle, *from a book by* Pierre Boulle. *Photography by* Jack Hildyard. *Music by* Malcolm Arnold. *Art direction by* Donald M. Ashton. *Film editor* Peter Taylor. *Sound by* John Cox and John Mitchell.

Cast: *Shears* William Holden. *Col. Nicholson* Alec Guinness. *Major Warden* Jack Hawkins. *Col. Saito* Sessue Hayakawa. *Maj. Clipton* James Donald. *Lt. Joyce* Geoffrey Horne. *Col. Green* Andre Morell. *Capt. Reeves* Peter Williams. *Maj. Hughes* John Boxer. *Grogan* Percy Herbert. *Baker* Harold Goodwin. *Nurse* Anne Sears. *Capt. Kanematsu* Henry Okawa. *Lt. Miura* K. Katsumota. *Yai* M. R. B. Chakrabandhu. *Siamese girls* Vilaiwan Seeboonreaung, Ngamta Suphaphongs, Javanart Punynchoti, and Kannikar Dowklee.

Hell Is for Heroes (Paramount, 1962)

Producer Henry Blanke. *Director* Don Siegel. *Story by* Robert Pirosh. *Screenplay by* Robert Pirosh and Richard Carr. *Director of photography* Harold Lipstein. *Special photographic effects by* John P. Fulton. *Music by* Leonard Rosenman. *Art direction by* Hal Pereira and Howard Richmond. *Set decoration by* Sam Comer and Robert Benton. *Film editor* Howard Smith. *Sound recording by* Philip Mitchell and John Wilkinson. *Makeup supervision by* Wally Westmore. *Assistant directors* William McGary and James Rosenberger. *Technical advisor* Maj. William Harrigan, Jr.

Cast: *Reece* Steve McQueen. *Corby* Bobby Darin. *Pike* Fess Parker. *Larkin* Harry Guardino. *Henshaw* James Coburn. *Kolinsky* Mike Kellin. *Capt. Loomis* Joseph Hoover. *Cumberly* Bill Mullikin. *Sgt. Frazer* L. Q. Jones. *Monique* Michelle Montau. *Capt. Mace* Don Haggarty. *Homer* Nick Adams. *Driscoll* Bob Newhart.

The Longest Day (20th Century-Fox, 1962)

Producer Darryl F. Zanuck. *Directors — British scenes* Ken Annakin; *American scenes* Andrew Marton and Gerd Oswald; *German scenes* Bernhard Wicki. *Direction supervised by* Darryl F. Zanuck. *Coordinator of battle scenes* Elmo Williams. *Screenplay by* Cornelius Ryan, *from a book by* Cornelius Ryan. *With additional scenes by* Romain Gary, James Jones, David Pursell and Jack Seddon. *Photography by* Jean Bourgoin, Henri Persin, Walter Wottitz and Guy Tabary (helicopter). *Music by* Maurice Jarre. *Thematic music by* Paul Anka, *arranged by* Mitch Miller. *Art direction by* Ted Aworth and Vincent Korda. *Film editor* Samuel Beetley. *Special effects by* Karl Baumgartner, Karl Helmer, Augie Lohman, Robert MacDonald and Alex Weldon.

Cast — The Americans: *Carl Vandervoort* John Wayne. *Gen. Cota* Robert Mitchum. *Gen. Roosevelt* Henry Fonda. *Gen. Gavin* Robert Ryan. *Commander* Rod Steiger. *U.S. Ranger* Robert Wagner. *Schultz* Richard Beymer. *Gen. Haines* Mel Ferrer. *Sgt. Fuller* Jeffrey Hunter. *Ranger* Paul Anka. *Pvt. Martini* Sal Mineo. *Pvt. Morris* Roddy McDowall. *Lt. Sheen* Stuart Whitman. *Col. Newton* Eddie Albert. *Gen. Barton* Edmund O'Brien. *Ranger* Fabian. *Pvt. Steele* Red Buttons. *Lt. Wilson* Tom Tryon. *Gen. Bedell Smith* Alexander Knox. *Ranger* Tommy Sands. *Capt. Frank* Ray Danton. *Gen. Eisenhower* Henry Grace. *Pvt. Harris* Mark Damon. *Pvt. Wilder* Dewey Martin. *Col. Caffey* John Crawford. *Williams* Ron Randell. *Gen. Bradley* Nicholas Stuart. *Rear Adm. Kirk* John Meillon.

Cast — The British: *RAF Pilot* Richard Burton. *Capt. Maud* Kenneth More. *Lord Lovat* Peter Lawford. *Maj. Howard* Richard Todd. *Gen. Parker* Leo Genn. *Padre* John Gregson. *Pvt. Flanagan* Sean Connery. *Briefing man* Jack Hedley.

Cast — The French: *Janine* Irina Demich.   *Mayor* Bourvil. *Bouilland* Jean-Louis Barrault. *Kieffer* Christian Marquand. *Mme. Barrault* Arletty. *Mother Superior* Madeleine Renaud. *Sgt. Montlaur* Georges Riviere. *Adm. Jaujard* Jean Servais. *Renaud* Georges Wilson.

Cast — The Germans: *Gen. Blumentritt* Curt Jurgens. *Marshall Rommel* Werner Hinz. *Marshal Rundstedt* Paul Hartmann. *Sgt. Kaffeeklatsch* Gerd Froebe. *Maj. Pluskat* Hans Christian Blech. *Gen. Pemsel* Wolfgang Preiss. *Lt. Col. Ocker* Peter Van Eyck. *Col. Priller* Heinz Reincke. *Gen. Marcks* Richard Munch. *Gen. Salmuth* Ernst Schroeder. *During* Karl Meisel.

The Great Escape (United Artists, 1963)

Producer John Sturges. *Director* John Sturges. *Screenplay by* James Clavell and W. R. Burnett, *based on the book by* Paul Brickhill. *Director of photography* Daniel Fapp. *Special effects by* Paul Pollard. *Music by* Elmer Bernstein. *Art direction by* Frenando Carrere. *Film editor* Ferris Webster. *Sound by* Harold Lewis. *Makeup by* Emile Lavigne. *Assistant to Mr. Sturges* Robert E. Relyea. *Assistant director* Jack N. Reddish. *Technical advisor* C. Wallace Floody, M.B.E.

Cast: *Hilts, the Cooler King* Steve McQueen. *Hendley, the*

Scrounger James Garner. *Bartlett, Bix X* Richard Attenborough. *Ramsey, senior British officer* James Donald. *Danny Velinski, the Tunnel King* Charles Bronson. *Blythe, the Forger* Donald Pleasance. *Sedgwick, the Manufacturer* James Coburn. *Ashley-Pitt, Dispersal* David McCallum. *MacDonald, Intelligence* Gordon Jackson. *Willie, the Tunnel King* John Leyton. **The Allied Officers:** *Ives, the Mole* Angus Lennie. *Cavendish, Surveyor* Nigel Stock. *Goff, the American* Jud Taylor. *Sorren, Security* William Russell. *Griffith, Tailor* Robert Desmond. *Nimmo, Diversion* Tom Adams. *Haynes, Diversion* Lawrence Montaigne. **The Germans:** *Von Luger, the Kommandant* Hannes Messemer. *Werner, Ferret* Robert Graf. *Strachwitz, Security Sgt.* Harry Riebauer. *Kuhn, Gestapo* Hans Reiser. *Posen, the Adjutant* Robert Freitag. *Kramer, Ferret* Heinz Weiss. *Frick, Ferret* Til Kiwe. *Preissen, Gestapo* Ulrich Beiger. *Dietrich, S.S.* George Mikell. *Steinach, S.S.* Karl Otto Alberty.

Patton (20th Century-Fox, 1970)

Producer Frank McCarthy *Director* Franklin J. Schaffner. *Screenplay by* Francis Ford Coppola and Edmund H. North. *Photography by* Fred Koenekamp. *Second unit camera* Clifford Stine and Cecilio Paniagua. *Music by* Jerry Goldsmith. *Art direction by* Urie McCleary and Gil Parrando. *Set decoration by* Antonio Mateos and Pierre-Louis Thevenet. *Film editor* Hugh S. Fowler. *Sound by* James Corcoran, Douglas Williams, Murray Spivack, Don Bassman and Ted Soderberg. *Assistant directors* Eli Dunn and Jose Lopez Rodero. *Second unit director* Michael Moore.

Cast: *Gen. George S. Patton, Jr.* George C. Scott. *Gen. Omar N. Bradley* Karl Malden. *Field Marshal Montgomery* Michael Bates. *Field Marshal Rommel* Karl Michael Vogler. *Gen. Bedell Smith* Edward Binns. *Col. Bell* Lawrence Dobkin. *Gen. Truscott* John Doucette. *Gen. Alfred Jodl* Richard Muench. *Capt. Steiger* Siegfried Rauch. *Col. Codman* Paul Stevens. *Capt. Jensen* Morgan Paull. *Slapped soldier* Tim Considine.

Index

225